CLARINET TECHNIQUE

Clarinet Technique

BY
FREDERICK THURSTON

1368

Second edition

London
OXFORD UNIVERSITY PRESS
NEW YORK   TORONTO
1964

Oxford University Press, Amen House, London E.C.4

GLASGOW NEW YORK TORONTO MELBOURNE WELLINGTON
BOMBAY CALCUTTA MADRAS KARACHI KUALA LUMPUR
CAPE TOWN IBADAN NAIROBI ACCRA

FIRST EDITION 1956
SECOND EDITION 1964

Printed in Great Britain by
The Camelot Press Ltd., London and Southampton

CONTENTS

PUBLISHER'S NOTE

The author of this book died while the MS. was in its final stages, and the publisher wishes to express his grateful thanks to Miss Thea King and Mr. John Warrack for their help in preparing the book for the printer and seeing it into print.

ACKNOWLEDGEMENTS

The illustrations showing correct and incorrect positions of the clarinet in the mouth are based, by permission, on an illustration which appeared in an article by Mr. Maurice M. Porter in the *British Dental Journal* of 5 August 1952.

The extract from Ravel's Septet is reproduced by permission of Durand & Cie., Paris (United Music Publishers, London); from Rimsky-Korsakov's *Coq d'Or* by permission of Rob. Forbert (Agents: Novello & Co. Ltd.); from Prokofiev's *Peter and the Wolf*, Rimsky-Korsakov's *Scheherazade*, and Gerald Finzi's Clarinet Concerto by permission of Boosey & Hawkes Ltd., the last-named work by permission also of Mr. Finzi; from Hindemith's Clarinet Concerto by permission of Schott & Co.; and from Elizabeth Maconchy's Clarinet Concertino by permission of Miss Maconchy.

FOREWORD

'The Clarinet has long been considered by the whole Musical Profession as the most beautiful of Wind Instruments. On the Continent it is very generally cultivated, nor is it improbable that in the course of a few years its merits will procure for it an equal degree of attachment from English Amateurs; for surely a Tone that nearly rivals the finest human Voice, and an extent of Octaves that may vie even with the ample range of the Violin, are excellencies that *must* at no very distant period share a considerable portion of popularity.'

So began Thomas Willman's *Instruction Book for the Clarinet* in 1825, and his prophecy has been more than fulfilled. Despite the many mechanical improvements the clarinet has enjoyed since his time, the aim of every player should still be, as Willman took pains to show, to develop a technique in order to serve his musical expression, and not as an end in itself. Anyone can, with diligent application, learn to control the mechanism of a clarinet; not everyone can play music on it. The former is no more than an efficient mechanic. Your technique must be good only because if it is not your musical expression will be impeded. There is no other reason for technique. Tone production, tongue and finger efficiency, choice of reed, and transposition are all a part of it, whether you are aspiring to play the clarinet, bass clarinet, basset horn, or saxophone; whether you intend to take part in chamber music, or to play in a symphony orchestra, a dance band, or a military band.

Even if you do not intend to become a professional, your enjoyment, and that of others, will be enhanced by technical efficiency. The adjective 'amateurish' should not imply 'incompetent'. The true amateur, in the dictionary sense of the word, is one who cultivates a particular study or art for the love of it; he is prepared to take trouble to be master of his hobby, and he is never despised by the best professional artists.

This book does not pretend to take the place of personal

supervision by a teacher; it can only give you the funda-
mental principles, perhaps in more detail than the average
space of the tutor or instruction book allows. It may be
helpful for those who cannot easily get first-hand instruction, but it should be used mainly to supplement your
lessons. Some regular tuition is essential if you hope to
become a fine player, if only because it is impossible to
describe on paper anything to do with beauty of sound.

Though the chapters may be taken in any order by more
advanced players, they may be followed straight through
by beginners. This order also corresponds roughly to the
ideal programme for a day's practice, although some of
its chapters are inseparable—for instance, those on tone
production and breathing, or articulation and staccato.
To avoid complication over fingerings for the various systems of clarinet still used, I have presumed that the player
has a chart to suit his instrument. A few of the remarks
apply to the Boehm only, as it is the most widely known,
but most of the examples should be workable on any
system.

NOTE ON THE SECOND EDITION

Since *Clarinet Technique* was first published in 1956, new
works involving the clarinet have appeared with astonishing
frequency, especially in the realm of music for chamber
ensemble. The list in Appendix III has been brought up to
date as far as possible and, although there can be no
guarantee that all works in print are included, it is hoped
that there are no major omissions.

Thea King

THE BEGINNINGS—TONE

You have chosen to play the clarinet because you are attracted to it and have a desire to produce yourself its particular kind of tone quality. All the books, all the articles and technical advice in the world are of little use unless you have in your 'mind's ear' the particular sound you wish to make. Presumably you will have decided this by listening to various fine players, if possible at public performances, because even nowadays the radio and the gramophone cannot reproduce tone quality completely faithfully. The nationality of the player or the make of instrument has little to do with it, whatever you may hear said; there are only two kinds of sound, good and bad.

Having selected what you think will be a satisfactory combination of reed and mouthpiece (see Appendices I and II) the first step is the foundation of a good embouchure, or necessary formation of the mouth, which includes the position and control of the jaws, lips, teeth, and surrounding muscles. The following remarks assume that you are a beginner, but even if you are not, it is a good plan to hark back occasionally over these preliminary points in the continual desire to improve your tone.

(a) Stand up straight with the body thoroughly relaxed, feet slightly apart, and head erect, looking straight ahead. It is best to play as much as possible standing up, but if you do have to sit down make sure that you adopt as upright a position as possible. Do not rest the bell of the clarinet on the knee as this is bad for the control of embouchure, fingers, and breath. Rather than resort to a sitting position because you are tired from playing, it is better to abandon practice until you are completely fresh, at any rate in the early stages. You will find, too, that a number of short spells of practice with short rests will keep you fresher than going on until you begin to tire and then resting until you feel ready to begin again. Five-minute periods will probably be found quite long enough at the very beginning: you will find your endurance developing of its own accord with time. But do not on any account over-practice: you cannot concentrate when you are physically and mentally tired, and you will do your playing as much harm as by not practising at all.

(*b*) Hold the clarinet with the right-hand thumb under the thumb-rest and the fingers of that hand resting against the rod attached to the rings. The left hand can be used to steady the instrument by holding the barrel. To produce the open note, G, none of the finger-holes need be covered. The elbows should neither be pressed against the body nor held out stiffly, but allowed to fall naturally. Positions of embouchure and stance obviously differ from one player to another, but the clarinet should make an angle of about 40° with the body.

(*c*) Put the tip of the mouthpiece between the almost closed lips and rest the reed on the bottom lip. Now gently push the instrument into the mouth so that the lower lip is drawn over the bottom teeth. Meanwhile let the top teeth rest lightly on the mouthpiece and close the lip around them, which will prevent any breath escaping when you actually blow. This shows you how to form the embouchure; so far you have produced no sound.

(*d*) First you must find out how much of the mouthpiece should be in the mouth to allow the reed to vibrate freely and give the fullest tone. So take a good[1] breath and then repeat (*c*), meanwhile blowing gently without puffing out the cheeks. At first you will get no sound at all, but as you push more mouthpiece into the mouth the note will suddenly come. Experiment gently with this, and you will find that there is a position which gives the most satisfactory sound. There should be a fair amount of pressure of the reed downwards on to the bottom lip. Now compare the position (in a mirror) with the diagram, which shows the average amount taken into the mouth by most first-class players. Practise this until you can take up the embouchure position quickly and comfortably. The sound

[1] For a fuller exposition of the problems of breathing and breath control see Chap. II.

you make at first may not be very pleasant, possibly for one of the following reasons:

(i) The reed may not be pressing firmly enough on the bottom lip. Your left hand, which is holding the barrel, can be used to test and adjust this at first.

(ii) The muscles from the corners of the mouth to the cheeks should be contracted as if in a forced smile, and there should be no air space between the inside of the cheeks and the back teeth.

(iii) When putting the instrument into your mouth, make sure that the clarinet goes to you, and not you to the

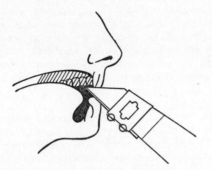

clarinet. Do not, for instance, take a sudden bite at the instrument.

(iv) Make sure, apropos the last point, that you are carefully following the instructions given in (c).

(v) Some players find it more comfortable to cover the upper teeth as well as the lower with the lip. There is nothing against this, but the other method is recommended as more generally satisfactory, and as being more likely to give an easy embouchure and consequently a good tone. The slightest change in position can make an enormous difference to the quality of the sound. You can only find out what suits you best by experiment. Obviously allowances must be made if you have protruding teeth, a very thick bottom lip, or a very long upper lip. There are sometimes instances of the teeth causing soreness or a cut lip. In extreme cases your dentist may help, but on no account resort to him without first consulting a clarinet teacher. There are one or two dentists in London with a specialist interest in wind players' problems. You may also find that the bottom teeth make a groove inside the lip, especially if they are sharp, but this will become easier with time; meanwhile it is wise to play for only short spells at a time.

Because the reed vibrates inside the mouth the size and depth of the cavity (or resonating chamber) must have some bearing on the quality and quantity of the tone produced. There are certain natural physical characteristics which help to make a fine player on any instrument, and in this case the formation of teeth, lips, and jaw doubtless has some effect. Many people try to play instruments for which they are physically quite unsuited, but a glance at the physiognomy of a number of fine performers will show that there is no such thing as a 'clarinet face'.

Long notes

When you feel that you can produce a reasonable sound on the open note, G, take your left hand from the barrel and play F, one tone lower (see your fingering chart); then go on lower down the instrument, gradually adding one finger at a time. Do not remove the clarinet from the mouth between the notes in case you should disturb the ideal embouchure position you have found. (If you do take the instrument out of your mouth and look at your fingering, be careful not to catch the reed on your left shoulder.) Merely relax the lips and take a breath through the sides of the mouth (*not* through the instrument). Start each note as quietly as possible, i.e. breathe very gently into the clarinet, and gradually increase the intensity of breath until you reach fortissimo (see Chapter II). Then diminish the tone back to the opening whisper, listening carefully so that the pitch of the note does not alter from beginning to end. If you try to force the tone too much the quality will suffer, the pitch will drop, or an unpleasant squeak may occur. At first you may not be capable of much variation in dynamics or a very long sustained note, but practice will extend this; in fact, this is one of the exercises you should be prepared to practise all your life, listening continually for a beautiful quality of tone.

Some notes on every clarinet are weaker in quality than others, noticeably the A and B♭ immediately above open G, the so-called 'throat notes'. This is because the keys and holes used to produce them are the highest up, so that there is only a comparatively short column of air vibrating in the upper part of the tube. Therefore special attention should be paid to these when practising long notes. Covering some of the right-hand finger-holes can help to improve the tone, but it must not alter the pitch (unless this is purposely intended for intonation reasons). Try to imagine also that you are increasing the mouth cavity to give more resonance to the note as in a yawn.

Where it is possible, for instance on the Boehm system, an alternative fingering for B♭ often gives a better note. With the A key, instead of the speaker use the second of the four trill keys, played with the right-hand forefinger (halfway up the instrument). This is particularly suitable if the B♭ has to be sustained for any length of time. It is too awkward to reach to be practicable in fast passages, but then the thinness of tone will not be so apparent and the normal fingering can be used.

II

BREATH CONTROL

The principles of good breath control in clarinet playing are fundamentally the same as those used in singing, although for some reason they are rarely considered in such detail by teachers of wind instruments. Specialists in voice production have written countless books on the subject, which are interesting for the clarinettist to study. A knowledgeable, factual, and unusually clear exposition is Franklyn Kelsey's *The Foundations of Singing*.

The aim should be to breathe as naturally and unconsciously as possible, with no more concentration on the mechanism involved than is needed when idly humming a tune. Most players find that breath control develops automatically as they advance. It can be a mistake to give too much thought to it while actually playing, though you should understand the muscles used in order to be able to control them at will.

In the normal, rather sedentary, life which civilized man now leads the lungs and breathing muscles are not often called upon to work at their fullest extent, and one only becomes conscious of how they function when 'out of breath' after violent physical exercise. The inhalation and exhalation of air is controlled by a very important muscle called the diaphragm, and not by the lungs, as most people suppose. This may be compared to a large piece of elastic forming the floor of the chest cavity and separating it from the abdomen. In a relaxed position it arches upwards into a dome beneath the ribs, the highest point being in the centre, and the lowest at about waist level. When contracted downwards the floor of the chest is lowered and the volume of the cavity between the diaphragm and the lungs enlarged. As this cavity has no outlet, a vacuum is formed, causing the lungs, suspended in the cavity, to fill out and correct the vacuum. As they fill out, they automatically draw in air from outside the body; this is simply what happens when you breathe in.

Then as the diaphragm expands upwards the air is forced out again, although the lungs are never completely emptied.

To appreciate how this muscle works, place your hand against the triangle formed (in the front of the chest) just beneath where the two lowest ribs branch away. Now breathe in as though you were going to heave a deep sigh or enjoy smelling a flower, and you will feel your hand being pushed outwards. This is exactly the way in which you must take a breath when playing the clarinet, although it will often have to be done more quickly. Practise first without the instrument until it becomes automatic. In other words, the *lowest* part of the lungs must be filled with air and you must not be tempted to raise the shoulders and use the upper part in an effort to snatch a quick breath between phrases. *Always* breathe from the very bottom of the lungs. Breathing from the shoulders will cause all the muscles of arms, hands, and fingers to stiffen, and relaxation is one of the first necessities when playing any instrument: if you are tensed-up physically more than is absolutely necessary your playing will be equally tense and uncomfortable to listen to. Quite apart from this, the air-stream when you breathe out again must be controlled from the diaphragm, which will be impossible if only the top portion of the lungs is filled. Whilst playing the clarinet the exhalation of air is obviously much slower than in normal breathing, and every scrap of it must be used to good advantage. Therefore practise inhaling deeply and fairly quickly and exhaling slowly and evenly, at first away from the instrument; then play some long notes (see Chapter I). By listening carefully to yourself you will be able to detect any jerkiness in the passage of air. Feel that the whole process is controlled from the diaphragm, which supports the air column and sends it straight through to the bell of the clarinet, the reed and the embouchure act-ing as sound-producers midway along the route, just as the vocal chords do in singing. It is especially helpful later when playing high notes or a really short staccato to notice this support and even tenseness of the diaphragm. Do not allow any tightening of the throat muscles. The faster the diaphragm is made to expel the air, the louder the note; and vice versa. Count a slow four from the start of the note to the loudest point, and another four until it dies away again. Remember to make sure that your body is thoroughly relaxed all the time, except of course for the vital embouchure and breathing muscles.

How often and when to breathe must be determined by the phrasing of the music, and of course individual breath capacities vary. No rules can be laid down; it is entirely up to the musicianship of the player and it cannot really be taught. Good breathing punctuates the musical phrases naturally, just as prose is divided into sentences or poetry into verses. An abnormally large breath capacity is not necessarily an advantage unless used with taste; in fact, there have been famous singers and players who managed with only one lung. However, there are certain places in clarinet music where one wishes that it were not necessary to make any break at all, for example in the opening twenty-four bars of the slow movement of Schubert's octet, and the long solo in the second movement of his Unfinished Symphony. Another difficult passage occurs in the slow movement of Brahms's second piano concerto:

This can trap the unsuspecting clarinettist, and is well worth studying.

Inexperienced players often make the mistake of letting the first breath last too long when they begin a piece just because they feel fresh. The result is that they feel quite exhausted for the rest of the piece, which will probably make the listener feel uncomfortable too. Try to space your breathing places as evenly as the music allows. If you find that you still have some breath left at the end of a phrase, get rid of it quickly before breathing in again. If you do not there will be a pocket of air in your lungs which is waste matter and very bad for you. Experience will teach you where to breathe, and playing to an audience or to some friends whenever possible is a help. Very often nervousness affects the breath control; then it is more than ever important to keep relaxed and to breathe deeply and freely, as this will have a soothing influence.

There are often 'danger spots' in certain works where it is best not to take a breath on any account, for example in the slow movement of Brahms's clarinet quintet:

If you breathe between these two phrases you may alter the embouchure slightly, and the note G may refuse to 'speak' at all, or it may suddenly jerk out mezzo-forte, which would be quite the opposite effect from what the composer intended. Try to reorganize the breathing points in the preceding and the following phrase so that you will not need to make a break here. Even in similar places where it *is* absolutely necessary to breathe before a pianissimo phrase, make sure that you hold the instrument quite still in the mouth during the silent beats. A good example of this occurs in Beethoven's Septet:

Try to avoid cutting off the last note of a phrase abruptly in order to take a quick breath for the next. There is *always* time to round it off, or to make the tiniest diminuendo. This is an important part of the art of phrasing, and it can be learnt only by example, not by precept. Listen carefully to a really fine artist on any instrument, and you will notice the little ebbs and flows of tone that go to make up his phrasing. These lie at the very heart of his artistry, and they are not to be explained by performers; only understood. Too many nuances spoil the line of a long phrase; too few make it dull. You must steer your own course between extremes; your teacher can point out some of the more dangerous rocks, but the actual navigation is in your hands.

III

ARTICULATION AND FINGER EXERCISES

As soon as you are able to play long notes confidently and with a full, rich tone, maintaining the pitch from beginning to end, the next step is to learn to use your tongue. This enables you to articulate, or give a clear and definite beginning to a note, as when pronouncing a word which starts with a consonant. Later the tongue is used to accent notes and for staccato playing (see Chapter VI).

Choose any note, say open G again, and play as for a long note, but on a sustained steady mezzo-forte. While doing this bring the tongue up to touch the tip of the reed gently and withdraw it again, repeating this several times.

You should find that the note reiterates, so:

in the same way that a string player interprets this marking; that is, playing all the notes in one bow, but with a little extra pressure of the bow on each. What actually happens on the clarinet is that the contact of the tongue with the reed momentarily causes it to stop vibrating, giving the articulation. You will find that there are several ways in which this can happen, but the most usual and most natural for most players is for the *tip* of the reed to touch the upper surface of the tongue about $\frac{1}{4}$ to $\frac{1}{2}$ inch away from its tip. You will find more details and a diagram in Chapter VI.

When you have mastered this, try actually beginning a note with the tongue, which should be in position against the reed as soon as you have taken a breath, and withdrawn as you blow, thus giving the note a firm 'edge'. When playing a series of articulated notes the repeated action of the tongue is similar to that used when pronouncing 'Da-da-da', one of the first sounds we utter from the cradle. There is no need to use force, because the tongue needs merely to brush the reed to stop it from vibrating. Practise articulating on each note you have learned so far, and you will be well on the way to a natural and easy staccato technique. Every musical phrase must be started in this way, except certain pianissimo ones, where it is best to approach it rather in the same way as the long notes already mentioned. A phrase usually ends with a natural diminuendo, or else with the expiration of breath, not with the tongue (but compare with staccato, Chapter VI).

Assuming that you can now obtain any note downwards from the B♭ above open G, try now to move the fingers whilst actually blowing. Make sure first that they cover the holes correctly, neither stiff and unbending, nor curled up as if clawing at the holes. I have seen both these positions with beginners. The centre of the soft pad of flesh on the underside of the end of each finger must be over the hole. To check this, hold the instrument (without blowing) and press the fingers down abnormally hard; then remove them and look quickly at the impression made by the rings and holes. Some beginners feel discomfort, even cramp, in the right hand after they have been playing for any length of time, which may be due to unsuitable placing of the thumb rest. If the discomfort does not disappear after some perseverance (playing in a relaxed way, of course) a slight adjustment can easily be made one way or the other.

It is generally most difficult to control the lifting of the fingers at first, so here is a technical exercise to help:

If you find it awkward to start at the bottom of the instrument because there are so many more holes to cover, take first the triplet beginning on C and then work downwards. Play each group eight times. Listen carefully to ensure that the tone is of the same quality which you produced

in long notes, and that the movement of fingers is not causing any unsteadiness of the mouthpiece. Make sure also
that each triplet is perfectly even in rhythm. Where there
are alternative fingerings for a note it is a good chance to
become familiar with them. Begin slowly, and as you get
more proficient play the exercise faster. The whole body
should feel relaxed, and the fingers must never stiffen in
an attempt to play rhythmically, nor should they be raised
far from the instrument. It is a good plan when playing
triplets in the right hand to imagine that the left is taking
all the weight of the clarinet, and vice versa: this encour-
ages light and free use of the moving fingers, as if you were
drumming them on a table.

When using the A ('throat note') key it is advisable to
touch only the lowest part of it with the nearest edge of
the left-hand first finger. You will see that it is specially
slanted so that it is easy to reach. In exercise (i) below
all that is needed is a gentle turn, squeeze, or roll of the
finger upwards; do not *lift* it from hole to key. Practise
very slowly and smoothly. Hardly any movement is necessary to uncover the hole and depress the key, although
the wrist may be allowed to turn slightly. The remaining
fingers of the left hand should not be allowed to stray far
from their holes or to huddle together nervously; try
anchoring them by covering the third (C) hole with the
third finger.

In exercise (ii) a similar action is needed for the left thumb,
and in exercise (iii) both first finger and thumb do it
together. Exs. (i) and (ii) are primarily for the Boehm
clarinet, but they should be tried on other systems even
though the notes will not sound satisfactory.

There is no limit to the finger exercises you can invent.
Here is one for left-hand freedom. Try to avoid any unnecessary movement.

Plenty more technical studies can be found in any tutor or book of technical studies. Exs. (i), (ii), and (iii) above are especially useful as they help in the next technical difficulty, 'crossing the break'.

IV

CROSSING THE BREAK.
HIGHER REGISTER

As any chart will show you, the notes above B♮ (throat note) are played by using again the fingerings of the low register, at the same time opening the speaker key with the left thumb. This takes you as far as the C an octave higher, after which various 'cross fingerings' are used.

Play first the lowest note E on the instrument. While sustaining it open the speaker key and *slightly* tighten the embouchure muscles, thus changing the note to the B a twelfth above.

Playing smoothly over the break

Playing from A to B [♪♪] involves bringing into

action simultaneously all the fingers of both hands. It is

similar to the interval [♪♪] , although more diffi-

cult as the speaker key must be opened in addition to the slight adjustment of embouchure. You may find it easier to play downwards over the break first:

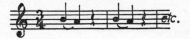

Remember the rolling action of the left-hand forefinger (see the last finger exercise in Chapter III). Now try playing upwards.

It is not absolutely necessary to raise all the fingers while playing the note A; the right hand, and even the third finger of the left hand, can remain undisturbed. This does not affect the intonation much on most clarinets, and even if it does, a little preliminary exercise can do no harm so long as you do not make a habit of it. Crossing the break smoothly is one of the major difficulties in clarinet playing, and you will see how important it is never to lift the fingers far from the instrument. When playing a passage which moves forward and backward from open G (or the throat notes) into the higher register it is often possible to leave the right-hand fingers in position throughout, especially if it is a fast passage. You must, of course, be able to play over the break *with* free use of all the fingers, so practise it both ways. This passage from the last movement of Mozart's concerto is notorious:

Allegro

Some beginners fall into the bad habit of stopping for breath, for instance in a scale, just at the point where it crosses the break, or of tonguing or articulating the difficult note, instead of playing it all as smoothly as possible. Try not to be cowardly: take a breath anywhere else, but not at this place, or you will be a long time in mastering this rather awkward technical point.

As you continue up the scale you will notice that the higher notes are more difficult to control, and it is not so easy to produce a clear, liquid quality. Practise long notes, listening carefully to the intonation; the pitch is likely to waver at first, and sometimes an 'undertone' (or another note) creeps into the pianissimo beginning of a note. This may be caused by one of two things:

(*a*) The embouchure needs adjusting. Considerably more tightening of the lip and cheek muscles is needed to support these notes, especially the high A, B, and C, and to give true intonation. 'Forcing the smile' more should help to prevent the note from sounding flat, or the quality from sounding 'wide'. At first the muscles may tire easily, and the fact that there are fewer fingers covering the holes as you go higher may make the instrument feel unsteady in the mouth, but plenty of practice will give you confidence. Experiment by starting the note mezzo-forte and diminishing it to piano, sustaining it for a few seconds, and then making a crescendo. If you can hold a steady pianissimo in this register you will be well on the way to a good control of the embouchure over the whole instrument. Do not be tempted to put more, or less, mouthpiece into the mouth; it may appear to solve the problem at first, but it will alter the tone quality, and obviously would be impossible if you were to meet a passage leaping quickly from high to low notes.

(*b*) The reed is unsuitable. A reed which is too soft needs more control when playing higher notes, and your embouchure muscles may not be flexible enough yet to give this. Try using a reed cutter (see Appendix II) or a slightly stiffer reed.

Intonation above the high C needs especial care. If you have trouble and are satisfied that your embouchure is not to blame, try using the alternative fingerings which are given in nearly every chart. No two clarinets give the same results in this register; if some of the notes sound flat, for instance, try using one of the right-hand little finger keys: probably the one normally used for Ab/Eb will help. You must find out which fingerings suit your particular instrument the best, checking the intonation by comparing the notes with the same ones an octave lower, as always.

Aim to be able to play any note on the clarinet with a perfectly controlled crescendo and diminuendo, as was said in the first chapter. Test yourself by taking them in any order, for example a high note followed immediately by the low E; or choose a note and play it in each possible octave. Listen all the time for a beautiful and even quality of sound and good intonation.

Leaps

Composers often ask the clarinettist to play wide intervals up or down in a short space of time, for instance at the opening of Brahms's F minor sonata, or in the first variation in the last movement of Mozart's quintet:

Allegretto

Naturally a certain amount of embouchure flexibility is needed, or else your playing will sound rough and out of tune. It is most helpful to try and hear mentally each note before you sound it, and to imagine the 'feel' of the embouchure you are going to use. Practise at first very slowly, as if it were a heartfelt Adagio, gradually increasing the speed each time until you eventually reach the correct tempo. This, by the way, is a good practice formula for all awkward technical passages. The following exercise is a good preparation, and you can invent many more to help in these kinds of difficulties:

V

SCALES AND ARPEGGIOS

Scales and arpeggios are the foundation of finger technique on any instrument, and you must be very patient in practising them, as they will help you to overcome most of the difficulties of clarinet playing. All classical works, and most post-classical works, are written in the diatonic system of major and minor keys, and so their melody and harmony are based on these principles. A scale is no more than a straight run up or down all the notes of the key the composer has selected and will be using constantly; an arpeggio is generally the notes of one or more chords in that key, played in series. The notes are, as it were, letters; the scales and arpeggios, in whole or in part, are words; and with them the composer writes his music.

As you read this page you do not stop at every word, add up the letters one by one, assemble their sound, and so pronounce the word, which then creates a mental image; your eye takes in the words at high speed, perhaps several at a time, and you understand them. This is because the technique of reading which you learnt in your earliest years has become second nature, which means in fact that your sub-conscious has been trained. You must now train the sub-conscious to read music on the clarinet as efficiently, so that when you see a row of notes going up the stave you do not take each one separately, name it to yourself, think of the fingering, play it, and then start work on the next note; your eye takes it all in, your brain registers 'scale of C major', and by that time your fingers have followed the brain apparently without thought and the passage is played. The ability to recognize scale and arpeggio patterns will also make your transposition more fluent. If you can instantly spot a series of notes as forming a chord of, say, D Major, you can then straightway think of it as E major and play it as easily as if E major were written down. Without this fluency you would have to think out every note, and would so be very much more likely to make mistakes. Of which more later, in Chapter VIII.

It might be held that with the gradual breakdown of the diatonic system in the late nineteenth and early twentieth centuries these arguments are out of date. This is not so: in the first place, there is happily no chance of classical works falling out of the repertory; in the second, you must adapt your scale practice to composers' demands. Practising whole tone scales, for example, will prove useful in the works of Debussy, and it might well be that practising tone-rows would be of value when sight-reading the music of Schönberg and the other twelve-note composers.

The performer must always be ready to adapt his technique to composers' requirements. This point will be returned to in Chapter VII. No one pretends that scale and arpeggio practice is anything but dull, hard work, but its eventual rewards are out of all proportion to the labour involved.

Scales

There are innumerable ways of learning to play scales, and it is best to have a book or tutor containing all the major and minor scales and arpeggios. Your choice may depend on the type of clarinet you play, but make sure that each scale covers the whole range of the instrument, and not just two octaves or so. There are some interesting French, Austrian, and Italian publications, but I favour the forms given in Bärmann's *Daily Studies for the Clarinet* because they are complete and concise and arranged rhythmically in bars.

With a little imagination endless variations in rhythm and articulation can be worked out, and you should play them pianissimo as well as forte, staccato as well as legato, and in as many different rhythms as you can think of. It is best to begin with legato so that you will hear immediately any unevenness; be conscious of each group of four notes and always play very rhythmically. Practise slowly and do not try to force the pace or your scales will sound uncontrolled; speed will come gradually. Play up and down each scale twice to give the fingers a chance to loosen and to encourage your breath control. Eventually you will be able to repeat it several times in one breath.

Here, for example, quoted from Bärmann, is C major, and two possible variants on it:

Interrupted scale:

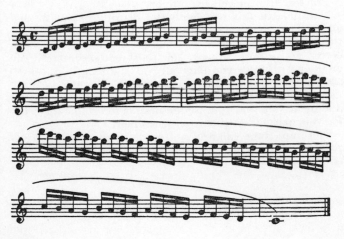

Scale in thirds:

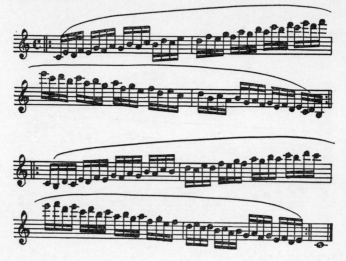

Practise also the relative minor.

Continue in this way with the diatonic scales through all the keys, starting with one sharp in the key signature, then with one flat, then two sharps, two flats, and so on. Never embark on a new key until you are thoroughly familiar with those you have already studied.

Chromatic scales use all the semitones consecutively. Practise throughout the whole range, again in varying rhythms, and make sure that you use the most comfortable fingerings for your particular system of instrument.

Here are some examples of rhythms in which you can practise scales. You can, of course, make up many more of your own.

Arpeggios

Try to play them evenly and with as little adjustment of embouchure as possible; make sure that the fingers are raised and dropped together or else the notes between the intervals will sound.

This figure is a useful one to practise as it takes you over each interval several times. As before, play in all major and minor keys.

Sevenths. So many passages containing dominant and diminished sevenths occur in clarinet music that you should be familiar with them technically.

Dominant seventh:

Diminished sevenths (of which there are only three):

This may seem a bewildering array for daily practice, but of course you can make a selection and work at it for a few days or a week, or choose a key involving some of the technical problems of the piece of music you happen to be studying at the moment. Above all, play always in strict time, and go back constantly over the scales and arpeggios you have already learned. If you have a thorough command over them you can face with confidence a black-looking run of semiquavers when sight-reading. And remember always to be relaxed.

VI

STACCATO

An easy and natural staccato is certainly one of the most important parts of the clarinettist's technical equipment. So many players regard tonguing as a stumbling block, but actually it is not difficult. Confusion usually arises because the teacher cannot see what is going on inside the pupil's mouth and does not bother to find out the exact position of the tongue in relation to the reed and mouthpiece.

Position

As soon as you were able to play long notes you learned to begin a note, or articulate, with the tongue. You will probably have discovered the best position for this at the time. As you are now going to concentrate on playing *short* notes in quick succession it is a good plan to re-examine it carefully. The shortness of the staccato note is governed by the speed with which the tongue returns to the reed to stop it vibrating. The most sensitive part of the reed is its tip, and this is also where the airstream is going to enter. Consequently you will get the best results if the tongue touches the *tip* of the reed.

Now try to find out which part of the tongue will contact the tip of the reed the most easily. While the tongue lies relaxed in the mouth its tip can be felt just behind the bottom teeth. When you put the mouthpiece into your mouth the tongue must merely be pushed slightly forward and upward to make contact with the tip of the reed.

You will probably feel the tip of the reed (and perhaps the tip of the mouthpiece) 'cutting' across your tongue about $\frac{1}{4}$ to $\frac{1}{2}$ inch away from its tip (on the upper and not the under surface, of course). I consider this the normal position for most players, although it is bound to vary according to facial structure, length of tongue, and so on. (See diagram overleaf.)

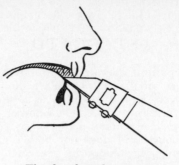

Tip of reed touches tongue

Playing short notes

Begin as in Chapter III with a long sustained open G divided into continuously reiterated sounds by the action of the tongue against the reed, and go on until you feel happy and certain that the tongue is working in the most comfortable way possible.

Now you can begin to aim at short notes for a true staccato, always starting from the long note, and having first taken a really good breath. Instead of merely brushing the reed and then withdrawing, as before, you must now leave your tongue in position against it, and then release it and replace it as quickly as possible. This will give you a short note. When your tongue returns to the reed for the first time you will only have used a fraction of that large breath, and the rest will be waiting in the lungs to be released down the instrument the moment you remove the tongue. Some of the air, but only a very little, may actually escape almost silently down the clarinet, because the tongue should not be pressed so firmly against the reed that it completely closes the aperture. Repeat this quick release-and-return action of the tongue until the whole breath is exhaled. There is nothing more to it.

Notice that it is the force with which the air rushes into the instrument when the tongue is taken away from the reed which gives a clear, crisp, staccato sound, and *not* the striking of the reed with any impetus. It is, in fact, the release of the tongue that produces the attack, not its return. Compare this with a toy balloon. If you pinch the opening tightly between finger and thumb, and then allow the air to escape in bursts by momentarily relaxing them, you will hear a series of puffs. The finger and thumb might be said to correspond to the tongue and reed, and the elasticity of the balloon to that of your diaphragm. The finger and thumb have nothing to do with the suddenness with which the air spurts from the balloon; it is the pressure of the air controlled by the rubber. You will see now the importance of having a large supply of breath ready to be expelled by the diaphragm. In staccato playing you will probably feel an extra tensing of the diaphragm and abdominal muscles, but in my opinion this is perfectly normal and correct, and can help to give more punch and point to your playing. All the other muscles (except of course the embouchure) must be thoroughly relaxed; this is essential if you are to develop any speed with the tongue. Be especially careful not to tighten the throat muscles.

Before going on to discuss speed, here are some warnings against common faults:

(*a*) Do not use the very tip of the tongue against the tip of the reed. This generally involves a certain contraction or contortion of the tongue, and causes unnecessary tightening of the muscles. A minor point is that the splayed tip of the tongue can wear out a good reed rather quickly (see diagram A on the next page).

(*b*) Do not strike the reed too far down, or with too large a part of the tongue's surface. This causes an unpleasant and clumsy sound (see diagram B).

(*c*) Do not tongue without touching the reed at all, either against the lower lip or against the roof of the mouth. Neither can give a really clean start to the note, and in the latter case the tongue has to perform such unnatural gymnastics that it cannot work freely. The less effort it makes the better.

(d) Do not expel or 'pump' the breath in short spasms with each note from the diaphragm. It is very exhausting, and of course impossible to do at any speed. It also makes the tongue lazy, because as the air ceases to flow into the instrument after each 'puff' in any case, it is no longer necessary for the tongue to return to the reed to stop the

INCORRECT POSITIONS

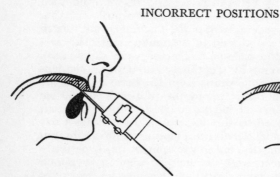

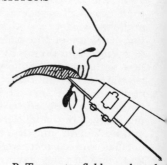

A. Tongue unnaturally stretched so that tip touches reed

B. Tongue too flabby and too low on reed

note. The control of exhalation from the diaphragm must be just as steady as when playing long notes or a legato phrase.

Learning to develop a fast staccato

As you increase the pace the silent 'gap' between the notes is going to become shorter and the tongue must work very quickly. You must therefore never withdraw it far from the reed. As you play faster its action approximates to that of 'du-du-du-du (u as in but) with a gentle d, except of course that the tongue touches the reed instead of the top teeth or the roof of the mouth. It is most useful to practise this away from the clarinet in your spare moments, for instance when out for a walk. Keep relaxed, as always, and your tongue will soon accustom itself to working fast. If you ask some of your friends who have never played a

wind instrument to do this you will find a surprising difference in their speeds. In the same way some clarinettists
find staccato easier than others do. Here are a few examples
of rhythm to practise, either on one note or away from the
instrument:

(useful in the 1st movement
of Beethoven's 7th Symphony)

When you feel satisfied about the position of the tongue
and can work it freely on one note at some speed, try playing scales and studies. If you find that certain notes 'miss'
or sound twice do not always blame your tongue. Perhaps
you are not raising or dropping your fingers absolutely
rhythmically or in co-ordination with the tongue. You
cannot achieve a good staccato in a few days; it needs
patience, but if you are willing to spend ten minutes a day
practising your facility will soon increase. You can test
yourself with a metronome every few days.

Take care that the embouchure is not forgotten, and
that the lip muscles function as in legato playing, the
tongue working quite independently. Very often the tone
quality suffers at first because the lip is slackened in an
effort to let the tongue move freely. This causes notes in
the upper register to sound flat, or an unpleasant 'undertone' to creep into them. Test yourself by playing the
passage legato first to make sure of intonation and quality,
and then, listening carefully, play it again staccato.

Finally, do not be downhearted if the results are at first
not encouraging, or if you hear the flute, oboe, or bassoon
in your orchestra playing a neat staccato with apparently
no trouble at all. Although it is difficult for them too,
I think it is easier than for the clarinet. Perhaps the wedge-
shaped mouthpiece, which forces the jaws apart more,
accounts for this.

Double and triple tonguing

This is not so common on the clarinet as on the flute,
but it is quite possible to cultivate the technique. Articulate

the consonants d-g d-g, or d-g-d d-g-d, as the case may be.

Double tonguing is useful for very rapid staccato passages, as in some Mozart and Rossini orchestral parts. It is also useful for repeated notes, as in the Introduction of Ravel's Septet:

Naturally synchronization of tongue and fingers is more than ever important.

It must be emphasized that double and triple tonguing should not be resorted to because your single tonguing is inefficient. Not only does a good single tongue sound clearer and cleaner, but there are certain critical speeds which are impossible for the double tonguer: they are too fast for his undeveloped single tongue technique, and too slow for double. The result is messy and uneven. By careful practice you can develop a single tongue that is very nearly as fast as a quick double tongue—and you will very seldom come across a passage requiring anything faster than that.

VII

TECHNICAL STUDIES AND FINGERING DIFFICULTIES

Your practice should include one or more studies from a tutor or book of studies, as this will help you to use and combine all the technical points already learned. Most of them are based on scales and arpeggios, articulated rhythms, or certain awkward sequences in remote keys. Unfortunately many are very dull musically and are apt to continue for pages in the same rhythm. Some of the extreme examples of the breed even have a patterned look, like wall paper. Try to avoid these; choose those which appeal to you and play them always as musically as you would any work in the repertoire, paying attention to the dynamics and phrasing. Many of Bach's unaccompanied string suites go well on the clarinet and make wonderful practice.

It would be impossible to mention a complete list here, but works by Bärmann, Stark, Jettel, Perier, and Uhl are all good. Especially recommended are Robert Stark's *Practical Staccato School* and Alfred Uhl's 48 *Etüden* (Schott).

Some of the most valuable studies are those which you can make up yourself around tricky passages in clarinet works. Always find out just where the difficulty lies, and which note is 'sticking'; do not be content to keep repeating the passage as it stands in the hope that it will improve if you go on for long enough. It won't.

As was mentioned in Chapter V, up to and including the works of Brahms there are very few instances of awkward technical passages which are not based on the various scales and arpeggios you are studying, but contemporary works often contain sequences which feel quite foreign to the fingers. As yet there are not enough books of studies in the modern idiom to help, so it is useful to be able to invent your own.

The following examples show you how to set about it, and they also give some alternative fingerings for use in special circumstances. There is no need to adhere rigidly to the fingerings given in your chart; as you advance you will probably discover new ones to help you over difficult passages. Always listen carefully for intonation, though, and be guided by your own taste. Never use a 'faked' fingering for a passage which you could play with the normal one after some practice. Do not be satisfied until you can play the notes backwards as well as forwards, and in any rhythm or tempo, or you will never feel safe with the passage, especially under the strain of performance.

In the following few selected cases I shall try to explain why each passage is difficult and to suggest ways of practising it. Naturally there are endless variations possible, so you must use your own ingenuity and develop the ideas to suit the work you are studying. Always play them in a set rhythm.

(1) Brahms's Quintet, second movement.

Difficulty: cross fingering, involving much raising and lowering of the fingers in a short space of time. Also, as it uses both the higher registers of the clarinet the embouchure must assist and the notes must be coaxed out.

(2) Cadenza from Rimsky-Korsakov's *Coq d'Or*.

Difficulty: continual breaking in the chromatic scale.

(a)

(b)

(3) Prokofiev's *Peter and the Wolf*.

Difficulty: unusual intervals, with the sequence rising chromatically.

(a)

(b)

(c)

(4) and (5). Here are two awkward passages for you to experiment with: the first is from the second movement of Hindemith's Concerto; and the second occurs at the opening of Elizabeth Maconchy's Concertino. Both contain unusual note sequences and intervals. The former is an excellent left-hand study.

(4)

(5)

(6) Here are two exercises for training the little fingers to find their keys easily.

Use the right-hand little finger throughout (Boehm).

Use the left-hand little finger throughout (Boehm).

The following fingering suggestions apply mainly to the Boehm clarinet, but the general principles and reasons for using them are the same for other systems. In any case, their suitability depends entirely upon the player and the instrument.

Choice of fingerings for B♭/B♮

(7) Opening of Weber's Concerto No. 1 in F minor. Provided that the intonation is satisfactory, use the first finger of the left hand with the second finger of the right (left thumb covering, as usual). In cantabile passages aim to make as little finger movement as possible so as to get a perfect slur.

(8) Mozart's Quintet, second movement; or indeed any passage involving an arpeggio of B♭. Use the first finger of the left hand with the first of the right. For both these examples the correspondence levers joining the two joints of the instrument must be perfectly adjusted or else the pads they operate will not cover well enough to produce the note.

(9) Mozart's Concerto, first movement. Use either the 'long' B♭ fingering as in (8) or the right-hand side key.

(10) Rimsky-Korsakov's *Scheherazade*; also in chromatic scales and in the diatonic scales of F and B♭. Use the left-hand (front) key, which gives neater finger movement and avoids synchronization of the two hands.

(11) Gerald Finzi's Concerto, second movement (written A♯ in the trill). Finger as for G♯, but lift the first finger, left hand. Intonation unsatisfactory, but hardly notice-able at speed, and in any case preferable to an uneven and clumsy movement with keys.

Additional fingerings for higher notes

For E♭ [musical notation] sustained for some time, or approached

by legato leap, try the following fingering:

Cover the second and third finger holes of the left hand, and third finger hole of the right hand. The little finger of the right hand opens the A♭/E♭ key.

But in chromatic passages, or for trilling with D beneath it, take the more usual fingering, covering the second and third holes in the left hand and first in the right (as for D), also depressing the small key between the second and third holes (right hand).

(Left thumb covers hole and opens speaker key for both these examples.)

The piano E ♪ which opens Busoni's Concertino

can be played on some instruments ♪ with the same

fingering as the throat A but with a tighter embouchure. The note can often be coaxed more easily from the instrument, but take care that the intonation is good and that the quality matches the following notes in the phrase.

All the notes in this region can be similarly overblown, but they must be used with discretion, and only in order to serve the phrase musically by avoiding jerky movements.

(12) Brahms's Quintet, third movement. Overblow the initial D from an open G. For similar passages involving C♯ (a semitone lower) overblow F♯.

 *etc.*

VIII

TRANSPOSITION AND SIGHT-READING

As you know, the commonest kinds of clarinet are the B♭ and the A. This means in effect that they are built a tone and a minor third respectively below normal pitch, and so the players' parts are written a tone and a minor third *higher* than normal in order to play at the same pitch as

everyone else. For example, if a flute fingers

it is that note which sounds; but if a B♭ clarinet fingers it

the note which sounds is . Therefore if the com-

poser wants his B♭ clarinet to *sound* C, he must write the note a tone higher in order to compensate, that is to say,

. Then, when the clarinettist fingers this D, the

required C will emerge. The note in the clarinet part has been moved, or, as we say, transposed.

Now this may seem to be going a long way round to get back to where you started. 'Why,' you may ask, 'can clarinets not be built in C?' The answer becomes clear when you hear the C clarinet—a squeaky little instrument, not without its special uses, but having none of the soft, mellow beauty which the larger bore gives the B♭ or A clarinets. The first clarinets were, in fact, in C, but it was found that B♭ or A were the two keys in which the instruments could be built most successfully. Beauty of tone is (rightly) preserved at the expense of a certain amount of bother.[1]

The point about having two clarinets is to make it easier. Suppose that the piece you are playing is in E major. To use the B♭ clarinet you would need a part written out in F♯ major, which has a key signature of six sharps. Not only in this unnecessarily tiresome to read, but an effect of the clarinet overblowing at the twelfth is to make the finger technique in extreme keys very much more difficult than it is comparatively on other instruments. If this part were written for A clarinet it would be in G major, i.e. only one sharp. A little thought will show you that pieces in a sharp key require the A clarinet, and pieces in a flat key require the B♭.

So far so good. But supposing, in an orchestral work, the music modulates from a sharp key to a flat one. The composer will then instruct you in your part to change instruments. But often you will come across parts written for C clarinet, and there is no hope for it then but to play on your B♭ or A instrument, transposing the part up a tone or a minor third as you go. This business of mental transposition may sound alarming at first. It needs practice, but it is a knack that can be learnt, and it is an essential part of the clarinettist's technique.

It is a good plan to include some transposition in your daily practice scheme. You must first of all get firmly fixed in your mind the new key signature; then try and play *in the key required* according to the shape of the phrase and the spacing of the intervals. To take a simple example: supposing you had to transpose up a tone the arpeggio of C major. First of all you would decide that the new key was D major, and then, recognizing the shape of the notes in front of you as a common chord, you should transpose it *as a whole* into the arpeggio of D major. Many

[1] Actually clarinets have been built in practically every key from A up to the A♭ clarinet, but the only one of the smaller instruments widely used is the E♭. Its music is written a minor third lower than it will actually sound. There are two instruments pitched lower than the normal A and B♭; the basset horn (in F, sounding a fifth lower than the written note) and the bass clarinet (in B♭, sounding a ninth lower than the written note).

passages can be treated in this way; try to avoid transposing each note separately up or down the required
interval.

C clarinet parts

Most players use the B♭ clarinet and transpose up a
tone, especially if the original has flats in the key signature, or perhaps one or two sharps. Accidentals must be
watched; very often a flat in the original becomes a natural
and a natural becomes a sharp. There is no easy rule of
thumb, but experience and musicianship will guide you.

If you read the bass clef easily you will find it best to
transpose extreme sharp keys (encountered, for instance,
in some Verdi C clarinet parts) on the A clarinet, reading
as for the bass clef. Here you must make sure that you
are playing in the correct octave (i.e. two octaves higher
than if it were in fact the bass clef), and mentally insert
the new key signature. Accidentals must be dealt with as
they occur.

Prelude to *La Traviata* (Verdi).

Excellent practice for such transposition can be found
in the earlier classical sonatas for violin and piano. Most
of them suit the range of the clarinet very well, and if you
have a partner at the piano it will encourage you not to
stop when you stumble over a note, as well as giving you
experience of works outside the clarinet repertoire. Even
string quartet parts can be used; compared to a stringed
instrument the clarinet has such a small field of chamber
music (although happily this is being remedied by modern
composers), that it is an excellent way of widening your
knowledge. The B♭ clarinet can take on viola parts with
success. This is done most simply by reading the alto
(viola) clef as if it were the bass clef, only one octave
higher.

D clarinet parts

As very few people possess a D clarinet, and there are not many instances where it is used, the part must be transposed down a semitone and played on the E♭ clarinet. A well-known example occurs in Strauss's *Till Eulenspiegel*.

Playing A clarinet parts on the B♭

This means transposing down a semitone, and is often convenient when the A clarinet is only wanted for a short time between two longer spells for the B♭. The slow movement of Brahms's first symphony contains a good example; technically it is perhaps even easier, and it does avoid having to pick up a cold instrument. As the clarinettist has two instruments to keep warmed up, it follows that intonation troubles are twice as bad for him as for other woodwind players, but facility in this kind of transposition will help.

Very often composers do not allow sufficient time for the player to change instruments, and then also it is necessary. Find a suitably long rest in your part, either before or after the change is indicated, and change clarinets there, transposing the intervening bars. This often happens between two numbers of an opera or a suite, for instance between the Introduction and the Allegro Vivo of Borodin's Polovtsian Dances from *Prince Igor*. Change well in advance, even omitting some of the *tutti* if necessary in order to be ready for the important solo which follows on the B♭ clarinet.

When transposing an A part down a semitone most players mentally substitute the new key signature, usually in terms of flats. Thus D major becomes D♭ major, and so on. Remember that in doing this the sharps in the original key will become naturals; and that the flats will become double flats.

When playing B♭ parts on the A, which is less common, this entire process is, of course, reversed.

Sight-reading

As in transposition, plenty of practice is the only way to get confidence and facility. If possible play with another person so that you will get a musical idea of the whole and not stop over details. Always look well ahead for any changes of time or key signature, and make sure about the tempo and dynamics before you begin by mentally singing or hearing the first phrase. Concentrate on getting the rhythm right: a few wrong notes will soon be forgotten even if they are noticed, but if you get the time wrong, even for a moment, you will falter and the chances are that the music will come to a standstill. Each time you practise finish by reading something new. There are some excellent books of selected orchestral passages for this purpose.

As you progress in your studies you will find yourself called upon to do more and more sight-reading, in orchestral and chamber work, or trying over new works with composers. It is one of the greatest tests of musicianship to be able to give a first-class impression of the musical idea and mood of a piece at sight, and it calls for every ounce of that equipment which we call clarinet technique.

APPENDIX I

PURCHASE AND CARE OF INSTRUMENT

When buying a clarinet make sure to get expert advice, particularly of course if you are a beginner and know nothing of the instrument. If you are already a player you may want to better your equipment, so here are a few hints on what to look for when buying an instrument. An expert should always be called in before the final choice is made; and no matter how expert you are yourself, a colleague's opinion is always of interest. You do not have to follow his advice.

The B♭ clarinet is the best to start with as on the whole it is used more often than the A, especially in the technically easier pieces. If you are interested in playing in a military band or a dance band it is essential. Later you may be able to find an A clarinet to match, or alternatively you can sell the B♭ and buy a pair.

Whether you decide on a new or a second-hand instrument:

(a) It must be low pitch. An old high pitch clarinet which has been converted by lengthening the tube will not do, whatever anyone tells you.

(b) The material must be good black ebony. Clarinets have been made from different kinds of metal, ivory, porcelain, ebonite, and plastic, but matured Mozambique ebony gives the best sound. The drawback about it is that it is sensitive to violent changes of atmosphere, and in extreme climates other materials have been found more satisfactory. Some instruments have bakelite bells and barrels, but the main body should be of wood, and there must naturally be no cracks. The most likely places for these to occur are round the holes, near the joints or near the pillars supporting rods and keys; always look carefully at these when considering an instrument for buying. The inside of the bore should be smooth.

(c) The keys should not be so soft that they can be easily bent with the hand. Springs and pads are not so important, as they can be replaced at comparatively low cost.

(d) The intonation should be good, and this is perhaps the most vital point of all. This means that the notes must be in tune with each other, in addition to the note A conforming to the standard pitch of 440 at a room temperature of 60°. Unfortunately there is no such thing as a wind instrument which is perfectly in tune. Also, a good clarinet may be thrown out of tune by using a mouthpiece of the wrong internal measurements; remember this when examining a second-hand one. Even two mouthpieces made by the same firm may give different intonation on any one instrument as the tonal chambers or internal measurements may not be similar, but some of the better ones have a serial number on each part so that no mistakes can be made. Mouthpieces are relatively quite cheap, and it is quite possible to have one specially made to suit the intonation of a good instrument.

System of fingering

Most eminent players now use the Boehm clarinet, although it is unfortunately the more expensive. Simple system clarinets can often be seen in shop windows for only a few pounds, but they are not always low pitched. At the time of writing prices for Boehm clarinets are:

A or B♭, first quality, new, £60–£80
A or B♭, first quality, second-hand, £45–£50
B♭, cheapest quality, new, £24–£28
(There is not always an A to match)
B♭, cheapest quality, second-hand, from £18

It is best to buy either a very expensive or a very cheap instrument; the former always has a market value if you ever want to make a change or give up playing, and with a cheap one your loss is negligible and more than compensated for by the hours of pleasure it has given. If someone offers to make you a present of a clarinet, accept gratefully! You can always check up on its points afterwards.

When buying a pair, see that they are matched, made by the same firm, and that the same mouthpiece fits and suits each. Obviously this is important for orchestral playing when one has to change instruments frequently.

Parts and care of clarinet

Starting from the base of the instrument the parts are:
  Bell
  Lower joint
  Upper joint
  Barrel, or socket
  Mouthpiece, to which is attached the reed by a ligature. This is usually of metal; German and Austrian players bind their reeds on with cord, but it is interesting to note that in these countries, where musical traditions are adhered to so strongly, the metal ligature is now beginning to be used.

Assembly. All joints are lapped with cork or cord, which should be kept slightly greased. The parts should be assembled with a twisting movement. If the joint is too stiff, grease it with a little Vaseline; if it is too loose, swell the cork by wetting or greasing it and then passing a match lightly underneath it. On some models particular care must be taken to see that the level projecting from the upper joint falls exactly over its counterpart on the lower joint. This ensures that the finger holes are in alignment and that the ring and pad mechanism receives correct and uniform pressure. In warm weather, or if the pitch of the clarinet rises a little after a prolonged spell of playing or in an overheated concert hall, the barrel can be unscrewed so that there is a slight gap between the outsides of it and the upper joint. This counteracts the sharpness, and it is therefore important that this joint should be kept in good condition and correctly greased.

Always leave the metal cap on the mouthpiece to protect the reed while you are assembling the instrument. Do not take it off until the last possible moment. The side with the reed attached must of course be in line with the back of the instrument, above the left-hand thumb hole and key and the right-hand thumb rest. Always replace the cap even if you only put the instrument down for a few minutes.

Springs and pads. The springs must be just strong enough to hold the keys down, ensuring that the hole is airtight, but not so strong that they impair the agility of the fingers. Keep them oiled, and also oil the key rods between the pillars, but see that none touches the pads. A light oil marketed under the name of '3-in-1' is suitable for this purpose. Skin pads are best, and they should be watched for any suspicion of leaking or becoming water-logged, and renewed when necessary. Otherwise an embarrassing gurgle may ruin a beautiful phrase! If you do suffer this misfortune, blow sharply across and into the hole. A piece of cigarette paper placed under the key will then absorb any surplus moisture. If you have recurrent trouble with water in the same hole, consult your teacher.

Bore. From time to time a light dampening of the bore with linseed oil is advisable. Put cigarette papers under the pads to protect them, and do it with a special cloth. Most important of all is the regular cleaning of the bore each time after playing, even if you have only been playing for a very short time. This is best done with a pull-through, similar to that used for rifles in the Army. It removes condensation, making the bore smooth and polished, and this in turn helps to improve the tone. It is, by the way, probably not true to say that a clarinet mellows and matures with age to the extent that a violin does, for instance.

The player must gradually adapt himself to his instrument and learn to get the best from it, always handling it carefully and keeping it in perfect working order. It is a good plan to have it completely overhauled every year or so.

CHOICE OF MOUTHPIECE AND REED

The mouthpiece is usually made of ebonite, and as the reed (which is flat) is placed against the opening, obviously the face of it must fall or curve away in order to leave an aperture through which the breath can enter and start the reed vibrating. There are many possibilities of the exact degree of slope, and different angles suit different players and types of playing. Research has shown remarkably little variation between the lays, or slopes, of eminent players' mouthpieces. A correct lay gives the resistance necessary to control the air flow and produce a real pianissimo or fortissimo. Consult a craftsman if you wish to check or re-lay your mouthpiece; he may have the measurements of some well-known players, which will help you to decide which is the best for you.

A close or medium lay tends to give a more refined, firmer sound with control of tone gradations; an open lay is more suitable for glissandos and vibrato. Of course, there are endless variations between the two. It depends a great deal on the player and the reed used, and here expert advice is invaluable. Once you have found a comfortable lay persevere with it; so many players do themselves more harm than good by constantly altering their lays, and consequently their embouchures, to say nothing of the time they waste.

Reeds

Plastic or cane can be used to make reeds, but so far the plastic reed has not been found satisfactory to the experienced musician playing chamber music, or for solo or orchestral work. This is unfortunate as it has the advantage of great lasting powers. Possibly in the future a composition reed will be produced which will give the good tone quality of cane and the long life of plastic, and then the clarinettist using a cane reed will be as rare as the violinist using a gut E string is now.

Unfortunately a good cane reed can only be selected by playing on it, and not by looking at it, so it is best to buy twenty-five or so at a time, or at the very least three or four. Then you can select the best for performing and perhaps use the others for practice. If a reed is transparent for some way down from the tip, thin and very flexible, it will be a soft reed; and a hard reed has the opposite features. For an untrained lip it is best to start with a fairly soft reed, but remember that if it is too soft the tone will be thin and weak. If it is too hard unnecessary effort will be needed to produce a note, which will be a harsh sound accompanied by air and a fluffy noise. It usually takes a little time before the reed feels settled on the mouth-piece, and its character can alter with use. The action of the tongue can make it thinner and softer, although some-times moisture hardens it. The same reed can feel and sound quite different on two different lays; usually a reed which suits a wide lay is too soft on a close lay, and vice versa. Make sure that you buy reeds which are correct for your particular mouthpiece, and not necessarily those re-commended by a friend, who may use quite a different lay.

The reed should be a good golden colour, with a fine even grain; a slightly greenish reed denotes immature cane. The best cane is grown in France, and reeds manufactured there are usually the finest. Especially good are those made by Vandoren. If you should happen to be in Paris try to visit Vandoren's to replenish your stock. The shop is in the rue Lepic, Paris (Montmartre). Or you can per-suade friends to bring some back for you. Some players make their own, but so far not to the extent in this country that oboe players do. Reeds are graded into boxes of soft, medium, and hard, but one can, and usually does, find a surprising selection of all grades in any one box, regard-less of its label. The quality of cane has deteriorated since the war because many of the bamboo plantations were cut down and the sticks used as camouflage for tanks and guns. Afterwards the cane had to be planted afresh, and there is good reason for believing that it is often cut and made into reeds nowadays before it is sufficiently seasoned.

Great care must be taken when affixing the reed to see that it sits absolutely straight and centrally on the face of the mouthpiece. It should be held with the thumb and first finger of the left hand and adjusted with the thumb

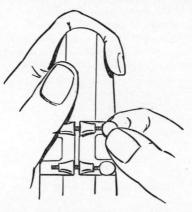

of the right hand. The normal position leaves a fraction of the mouthpiece showing above the reed, little more than a black line when looking at the instrument held vertically. If the reed is inclined to be too soft it should be placed a little higher so as to give more resistance; if it is too hard, place it a little lower. These adjustments must be only slight.

When a reed is too thin, and gives insufficient resistance, as often happens when it has been played for some time, a reed cutter can be used to clip a little off the tip and so stiffen it. If it has too much resistance it can be scraped carefully with a very sharp knife or razor blade on the shaded part of the reed (as illustrated).

Sometimes, after a reed has been played for some time it seems to lose its resilience, and feels unresponsive to the tongue. You can help matters by inserting, very carefully, a piece of stiff paper or card, about the thickness of a postcard, between the reed and the mouthpiece. Gently ease it downwards so that it separates the reed from the mouthpiece a little. Remove it carefully.

These devices cannot be relied upon to improve a reed. It is primarily the quality of cane which produces a fine sound, and without a first-class reed it is impossible to give a beautiful and sensitive performance.

APPENDIX III

A LIST OF MUSIC FOR THE CLARINET

NOTE

All works which are known to the compilers have been included in this list. It does not, however, follow from this that the list is complete, and readers must not be surprised if works known to them have been omitted. Any additions which they may suggest will be noted with pleasure for inclusion in future impressions.

As far as possible the name of the original publisher has been given. The English reader will find that most foreign publishers have London agents, and that there is no need to ask for copies direct from abroad. Chesters and United Music Publishers between them represent most French publishers, and Chesters also have Scandinavian connections; Hinrichsen and Musica Rara represent a number of other European publishers; and other agents include Schott, Lengnick, and Augener (Galliard). Any good music dealer will be able to give advice on this matter.

The term 'MS.' followed by the name of a publisher indicates that copies of the work are available on hire only. The term 'U.S.' refers to works which are listed in library catalogues at the U.S. Information Service, 41 Grosvenor Square, London W.1.

Inclusion of a work in this list does not necessarily imply that it is in print.

The list is arranged as follows:

Clarinet and piano, or unaccompanied clarinet
Clarinet concertos
Clarinet and other wind instruments with or without piano and double bass
Clarinet with strings, other wind instruments and piano
Voice with clarinet, with or without other instruments

ABBREVIATIONS

A.M.P.	Allied Music Publishers
B. & H.	Boosey and Hawkes
Br. & H.	Breitkopf and Härtel
Ed. Russe	Edition Russe

M.R.	Musica Rara		
O.U.P.	Oxford University Press		
S. & B.	Stainer and Bell		
U.E.	Universal Edition		
U.M.P.	United Music Publishers		
U.S.	See note on page 51		

cl.	clarinet	vc.	violoncello
bcl.	bass clarinet	db.	double-bass
fl.	flute	pf.	pianoforte
picc.	piccolo	hp.	harp
ob.	oboe	str. qt.	string quartet
cor ang.	cor anglais	str. orch.	string orchestra
bn.	bassoon	perc.	percussion
hn.	horn	wind quint.	wind quintet, con-
trpt.	trumpet		sisting of flute,
tromb.	trombone		oboe, clarinet,
vn.	violin		horn, bassoon
va.	viola	arr.	arrangement
		cont.	contemporary
		ed.	edited by

CLARINET AND PIANO, OR
UNACCOMPANIED CLARINET
(the former unless otherwise stated)

ABSENGER: Vortragstücke (*Br. & H.*)

AKIMENKO, T. (1876–1945): Op. 19 Petite Ballade (*Belaieff*); Petite Poème (*Jurgenson*)

ALBÉNIZ, I. (1860–1909): Chant d'Amour (*Leduc*)

ALWYN, WILLIAM (b. 1905): Sonata (1962) (*B. & H.*)

AMELLER (cont. French): Cantilène (*Leduc*)

ANTJUFEJEW, G.: Two Pieces (*M.R.*)

APOSTEL, H. E. (b. 1901): Op. 19 No. 2 Sonatina for unaccomp. cl. (*U.E.*)

ARMITAGE, IRENE: Dance Suite (*New Wind Music*)

ARNELL, RICHARD (b. 1917): Eight Pieces (*Hinrichsen*)

ARNOLD, MALCOLM (b. 1921): Sonatina (*Lengnick*)

ASHTON, ALGERNON (1859–1937): Tarantella (*Hofbauer*)

BABIN, VICTOR (b. 1908): Divertissement Aspenois (unaccomp.) (*Augener*); Hillandale Waltzes (*B. & H.*)

BACEWIZ, GRAZYNA (b. 1909): Latwe Utwory (*Polish State Publishing House*); Latvian Dances (*M.R.*)

BALFOUR, BETTY (cont. British): Three Highland Sketches, 1938
   (*B. & H.*)
BARAT, J. (cont. French): Pieces include Fantasie Romantique
   (*Leduc*)
BARBIER, RENÉ: Allegro Brillante (*Editions Brogneaux, Brussels*)
BARILLER, R. (cont. French): Arlequinada (*Leduc*)
BARNETT, DAVID: Fantasy on a Spanish Folk-song (*Salabert*)
BARRAINE, ELSA (b. 1910): Serenade (*Editions Ch. Gras, Paris*)
BAUSSNERN, WALDEMAR VON (1866–1931): Suite No. 3 (*Vieweg
   Berlin-Lichterfelde*)
BAX, ARNOLD (1883–1953): Sonata (*Chappell*)
BEAUCAMP, A. (cont. French): Complainte (*Leduc*)
BENJAMIN, ARTHUR (1893–1960): Le Tombeau de Ravel (Valse-
   Caprices) (*B. & H.*)
BENTZON, JORGEN (1897–1948): Op. 14 Theme and Variations
   (unaccomp.) (*Hansen*)
BERG, ALBAN (1885–1935): Op. 5 Four Pieces (*U.E.*)
BERNARD, JAMES (b. 1925): Sonatina (*O.U.P.*)
BERNSTEIN, LEONARD (b. 1918): Sonata (*Witmark, New York*)
BITSCH, M. (cont. French): Pièce Romantique (*Leduc*)
BLÉMANT, L. (cont. French): Bolero (*Leduc*)
BLYTON, CAREY: Scherzo (*New Wind Music*)
BOISDEFFRE, R. DE (1838–1906): Op. 12 Sonata (*Hamelle*); Op.
   20 Trois Pièces (*U.M.P.*)
BONNEAU, P. (cont. French): Suite in 4 movements (*Leduc*)
LE BOUCHER (cont. French): Ballade (*Costallat*)
BOURNONVILLE (cont. French): Fantasie Impromptu (*Costallat*)
BOWEN, YORK (1884–1961): Sonata (*MS.*)
BOZZA, EUGENE (cont. French): Pieces include Bucolique, 1949
   (*Leduc*)
BRAHMS, JOHANNES (1833–97): Op. 120, Nos. 1 and 2 Two
   Sonatas
BRÉARD (cont. French): Primesant (*Leduc*)
BROWNE, PHILIP (cont. British): A Truro Maggot, 1944 (*B. & H.*)
BRUNS, VICTOR: Op. 22 Sonata (*Pro Musica, Leipzig*)
BUMCKE, G.: Op. 9 Sonata, 1905 (*Simon*)
BURGMÜLLER, N. (1810–36): Sonata (*Kistner*)
BUSONI, FERRUCIO (1866–1924): Elegie (*Br. & H.*)
BUSSER, HENRI (b. 1872): Op. 72 Pieces include Cantegril
   (*Leduc*)
BUTTERWORTH, NEIL (b. 1934): Pastorale (*New Wind Music*)
BYRNE, ANDREW (b. 1925): Two Pieces (*Hinrichsen*)
CAHUZAC, LOUIS (cont. French): Fantasie Variée (*Hansen*)
CAPLET, ANDRÉ (1878–1925): Improvisations (*Durand*)

E

CARDEW, PHIL: Scherzo (*B. & H.*); The Lazy Faun (*New Wind Music*)

CASTRO, JOSÉ MARIA (b. 1892): Tres Piezas (*Ed. Argentina Musica*)

CAVALLINI, E. (1807–1874): Elégie (*Ricordi*)

CHAGRIN, FRANCIS (b. 1905): Improvisation and Toccatina (unaccomp.) (*Augener*)

CLERISSE, ROBERT (cont. French): Pieces include Promenade (*Leduc*)

CLIFTON, CHALMERS: Intermezzo and Humoresque, 1926 (*Le Roy*)

COOKE, ARNOLD (b. 1906): Alla Marcia (*O.U.P.*) Sonata (*Novello*)

COWELL, HENRY (b. 1897): Three Ostinati with Chorale (*Music Press Inc., New York*)

COX, DAVID: Shalemy Dance (*O.U.P.*)

CRUFT, ADRIAN (b. 1921): Op. 22 Impromptu (*Joseph Williams*)

CUI, C. (1835–1918): En partant (*Leduc*)

DAUTREMER, M. (cont. French): Récit et Impromptu (*Leduc*)

DEBUSSY, CLAUDE (1862–1918): Petite Pièce (*Durand*)

DÉSENCLOS, A. (cont. French): D'un Troubadour (*Leduc*)

DEVREESE, G. (b. 1893): Rhapsodie (*Gervan*)

DEWANGER, ANTON (cont. French): Op. 88 Ballade, 1954 (*Leduc*)

DODD, RAYMOND (b. 1929): Prelude, Air, and Scherzo (*O.U.P.*)

DONATO, VINCENZO DI (b. 1887): Pastorale (*de Santis*)

DONNINGTON, MARY (1877–1946): Prelude and Gavotte (*Joseph Williams*)

DRIESSLER: Op. 24, No. 3a Five Pieces (*U.E.*)

DUKAS, PAUL (1865–1935): Alla Gitana (*Leduc*)

DUNHILL, THOMAS (1877–1946): Op. 91 Phantasy Suite (*B. & H.*)

EDMUNDS, CHRISTOPHER (b. 1899): Gay Hornpipe; Highland Croon; Lament (*Schott*)

ELLIS, B. KOHS: Sonata (*Mercury*)

EXTON, JOHN (cont. British): Sonata (*MS.*)

FAERBER, O.: Op. 26 Sonata (*M.R.*)

FERGUSON, HOWARD (b. 1908): Four Short Pieces (*B. & H.*)

FERLING (cont. French): Adagio (*Leduc*)

FIBICH, ZDENĚK (1850–1900): Op. 16 Selanka (*Urbanek, Prague*)

FINCH, R.: Romance (*Chester*)

FINKE, F. F.: Sonata (*M.R.*)

FINZI, GERALD (b. 1901): Five Bagatelles (*B. & H.*)

FLOSMAN, O.: Sonata (*M.R.*)

FLOTHUIS, MARIUS (b. 1914): Kleine Suite (*Donemus*)

FRID, GÉZA (b. 1904): Op. 42 Rhapsodie (*Donemus*)

FRIEMAN, W. (b. 1889): Sonata (*Polish State Publishing House*)

FRISKIN, JAMES (b. 1886): Elegy (*S. & B.*)

FRUGATTA, G.: Suite de 6 Pezzi (*Ricordi*)

FULTON, NORMAN (b. 1909): Three Movements (*Augener*)
GABRIEL-MARIE (cont. French): La Cinquantaine (*Costallat*)
GADE, NIELS (1817–90): Phantasy Pieces (*Augener*)
GAGNEBIN, H. (b. 1886): Andante and Allegro (*Leduc*)
GALLOIS, MONTBRUN, R. (cont. French): Pieces include Concertstück (*U.M.P.*)
GAUBERT, PHILIPPE (1879–1941): Pieces include Fantasie (*Heugel*)
GEISSLER, F.: Sonata 1954 (*M.R.*)
GERMAN, EDWARD (1863–1936): Romance (*Rudall Carte*); Pastorale and Bourée (*Rudall Carte*); Song without words (*Augener*); Andante and Tarantella (*Rudall Carte*)
GIBBS, C. ARMSTRONG (1889–1960): Three Pieces (*O.U.P.*)
GILSON, PAUL (1865–1942): Pièces Romantiques (*Gervan*)
GIPPS, RUTH (b. 1921): The Kelpie of Corrievreckan (*Hinrichsen*); Prelude (unaccomp.) (*Joseph Williams*)
GLIÈRE, R. (b. 1875): Deux morçeaux (*Jurgenson*)
GOATLEY, ALMA: Summer Evening at Bryanston (*B. & H.*)
GODARD (cont. French): Op. 116 Allegretto (*Durand*)
GOEDICKE, A. F. (b. 1877): Zwei Stücke (*U.E.*)
GOEHR, ALEXANDER (b. 1932): Op. 3 Fantasias (*Schott*)
GOEYENS, F.: Chant Moresque (*Hinrichsen*); Arioso (*Hinrichsen*)
GOLESTAN, STAN (b. 1875): Eclogue (*Salabert*)
GOULD, MORTON (b. 1913): Guajira (*Chappell*)
GOUVY, T. (1819–98): Op. 67 Sonata (*Richault*)
GOW, DAVID (cont. British): Three Miniatures (*Augener*)
GRETCHANINOFF, A. (b. 1864): Suite Miniature (10 Easy Pieces) (*Leduc*); Sonata No. 2 (*U.S.S.R. State Music*)
GROVLEZ, GABRIEL (1879–1944): Lamento et Tarantelle (*Leduc*)
GRUDIN, V.: Op. 13 Two Pieces (*U.S.S.R. State Music*)
HAHN, REYNALDO (1875–1947): Sarabande et Thème Variée (*Heugel*)
HAMILTON, IAIN (b. 1922): Sonata (*Schott*); Three Nocturnes (*Schott*)
HARRISON, PAMELA (cont. British): Sonata (*MS.*)
HARTIG, H. F.: Op. 7 Sonata, 1952 (*Bote & Bock*)
HEAD, MICHAEL (b. 1900): Echo Valley (*B. & H.*)
HEAP, C. S. (1847–1900): Sonata (*Br. & H.*)
HEIDEN, B.: Sonatine (*M.R.*)
HILL, E. BURLING-HAME (b. 1872): Op. 32 Sonata (*Schirmer*)
HINDEMITH, PAUL (b. 1895): Sonata (*Schott*)
HODDINOTT, ALUN (b. 1929): Sonatina (*MS.*)
HOLBROOKE, J. (b. 1878): Andante and Presto (*B. & H.*); Op. 55, No. 8 Four Mezzotints (*Cary*); Nocturne Phrine (*Modern Music Library*)

HOLMÉS, A. (1847–1903): Fantaisie (*Leduc*)

HONEGGER, A. (1892–1955): Sonatine (*Salabert*)

D'HOOGHE, C. L.: Flemish Ballade (*Metropolis*)

HOPKINS, ANTONY (b. 1921): Fantasy (*Chester*)

HORDER, MERVYN: Theme with 6 Short Variations (*Hinrichsen*)

HOROVITZ, JOSEPH (b. 1926): Two Majorcan Pieces (*Mills*)

HOWELLS, HERBERT (b. 1892): Sonata (*B. & H.*)

HUGON, G. (cont. French): Scherzo, 1951 (*Costallat*)

HUNT, REGINALD: Meditation (*B. & H.*)

HURLSTONE, WILLIAM (1876–1906): Four Characteristic Pieces (*Cary*)

ILIFF, JAMES (cont. British): Three Characteristic Pieces (*MS.*)

IRELAND, JOHN (b. 1879): Fantasy-Sonata (*B. & H.*)

JACOB, GORDON (b. 1895): Sonatina (*Novello*)

JEANJEAN, PAUL (cont. French): Pieces include Prélude et Scherzo (*Leduc*)

JELESCU, PAUL (cont. Rumanian): Suite (*Rumanian State Publishing House*)

JENNER, G.: Op. 5 Sonata, 1900 (*Br. & H.*)

JETTEL, RUDY (cont. Austrian): Introduction and variations on an original theme (pf. or orch.) (*Kliment*); Sonata (*Hofmeister*)

JONGEN, J. (1873–1953): Sonata (*Chester*)

JUON, PAUL (1872–1940): Op. 82 Sonata (*Schlesinger*)

KARG-ELERT, S. (1877–1933): Op. 139*b* Sonata (*Zimmermann*); Op. 110 Sonata for solo cl. (*Zimmermann*)

KENDELL, IAIN: Episode (*Chester*)

KEENAWAY, LAMONT (cont. British): Caprice (*Schott*)

KLOSÉ, H. (1808–80): Pieces include Concertino (*Leduc*)

KOECHLIN, C. (1867–1951): Op. 178 14 Pieces (*MS.*); Two Sonatas (*MS., Oiseau Lyre*); Op. 215 Monodies for solo cl. (*MS.*)

KORNAUTH, EGON (b. 1891): Op. 3 Sonata (*Döblinger*); Op. 5 Sonata (*Zimmermann*)

KORTCHMAREV, K. A.: Two Pieces (*U.S.S.R. State Music*)

KREJKI (b. 1904): Sonatine (*Artia*)

KRENEK, ERNST (b. 1900): Monologue (unaccomp.) (*U.E.*); Suite (*Schott*)

LADERMAN, E.: Serenade (unaccomp.) (*M.R.*)

LADMIRAULT, P. (1877–1944): Sonata (*Leduc*)

LAPARRA, R. (1876–1943): Prélude, Valse et Irish Reel (*Leduc*)

LAURISCHKUS, M. (1876–1929): Op. 4 (*Simon*) and Op. 30 Miniaturen (*Simrock*)

LECAIL (cont. French): Fantaisie Concertante (*Leduc*)

LEFÉBVRE, CHARLES (1843–1917): Fantaisie Caprice (*Leduc*)

LEFÉVRE, XAVIER (1763–1829): 3me and 5me Sonate (*Richli*)

LEROUX, X. (1863–1919): Un Soirée près du Lac (*Heugel*)

LITAIZE, G. (cont. French): Récitatif et Thème Variée (*Leduc*)

LLOYD, CHARLES (1849–1919): Suite in the Olden Style (*B. & H.*)

LOTHAR: Op. 74 Sonata (*U.E.*)

LUCAS, C. (1866–1947): Divertissement (*Durand*)

LUCAS, M. A. (1882–1952): Sonata (*Hinrichsen*); Rhapsody (*Hinrichsen*); Lament (*Hinrichsen*)

LUTOSLAWSKI W.: Preludia (*Polish State Publishing House*)

LUTYENS, ELISABETH (b. 1906): Op. 14, No. 1 Five Pieces (*MS.*); In Memoriam (*MS.*); Op. 28 Valediction (*MS.*)

MAGNANI, A. (cont. French): Mazurka-Caprice (*Leduc*)

MAHY, A: Poème (*Gervan*)

MARTELLI, H. (b. 1895): Préambule et Scherzo (*Costallat*)

MARTINU, BOHUSLAV (1890–1959): Sonatina (*Leduc*)

MARTY, G. (1860–1908): Fantaisie (*Leduc*)

MASON, D. G. (1873–1953): Op. 14 Sonata (*Schirmer*)

MATHIAS, WILLIAM (b. 1934): Sonata (*Mills*)

MAWET, LUCIEN: Pièce Lyrique (*Evette & Schaffer*)

MAXFIELD, RICHARD: Two Sonatas (*MS.*)

MAYER, JOHN: Raga Music (unaccomp.) (*Lengnick*)

MAZELLIER, J. (b. 1879): Fantaisie Ballet (*Leduc*)

MENDELSSOHN, F. (1809–47): Sonata (*Schirmer*)

MESSAGER, A. (1853–1929): Solo de Concours (*Leduc*)

MEULEMANS, A. (b. 1884): Rhapsodie (*Gervan*)

MIHALOVICI (b. 1898): Sonata (*U.M.P.*)

MILFORD, ROBIN (1903–59): Lyrical Movement (*O.U.P.*)

MILHAUD, DARIUS (b. 1892): Sonatine (*Durand*); Duo Concertant (*Heugel*)

MIRANDOLLE, L. (cont. French): Sonata (*Leduc*); Sonatine (*Leduc*)

MIROUZE, M. (cont. French): Humoresque (*Leduc*)

MOESCHINGER, A. (b. 1897): Op. 65 Sonatina (*B. & H.*)

MOUQUET, J. (cont. French): Solo de Concours (*Leduc*)

MULDER, HERMANN: Sonata No. 3 (*Donemus*)

MULLER, HERMANN: Petite Sonate (*Edition Henn, Geneva*)

MURRILL, HERBERT (1909–52): Prelude, Cadenza, and Fugue (*O.U.P.*)

NICOLOV, LAZAR: Four Little Pieces (*M.R.*)

NORTH, ROGER (cont. British): Sonata (*Chester*)

D'OLLONE, M. (b. 1875): Fantaisie Orientale (*Leduc*)

OSBORNE, WILLSON: Rhapsody (unaccomp.) (*Hinrichsen*)

OSIECK, HANS (b. 1910) Sonatine (*Donemus*)

OSORIO-SWABB, REINE: Sonatine for Cl. 1946 (unaccomp.) (*Donemus*)

OUBRADOUS, F. (cont. French): Cadence et Divertissement (*Oiseau Lyre*)

PARROTT, IAN (b. 1916): Aquarelle (*Chester*)

PERMINOV, L.: Ballade (*Leeds Music Corp., U.S.A.*)

PFEIFFER, HUBERT: Music for Unaccomp. Clarinet (Prelude, Scherzo, and Fugue) (*Lienau*)

PHILLIPS, GORDON (cont. British): Air (*Schott*)

PIERNÉ, G. (1863–1937): Pieces include Canzonetta (*Leduc*)

PIGGOT, PATRICK (cont. British): Fantasy (*Leduc*); Fantasia in E flat (*Leduc*)

PIRANI, MAX (b. 1898): Idyll (*Augener*)

PITFIELD, THOMAS B. (b. 1903): Conversation Piece (*O.U.P.*)

POBJOY, V. (b. 1908): Four Pieces (*Schott*)

POLDOWSKI (1880–1932): Pastorale (Clarinet in C) (*Chester*)

POOT, MARCEL (b. 1901): Ballade (*Vriamont, Brussels*)

POULENC, FRANCIS (1899–1963): Sonata (*Chester*)

PRATT, A.: Idylle printanière, 1913 (*Hawkes*); Souvenir d'Ispa han (*B. & H.*)

PROUT, E. (1835–1909): Op. 26 Sonata (*Augener*)

RAFTER, LEONARD: Five Satires (*Bosworth*)

RAINIER, PRIAULX (b. 1903): Suite (*Schott*)

RAKOV, N.: Sonata (*M.R.*)

RAPHAEL, GÜNTHER (b. 1903): Op. 65 III Sonatine (*Br. & H., Wiesbaden*)

RAYBOULD, CLARENCE (b. 1886): The Wistful Shepherd (*B. & H.*)

REGER, MAX (1873–1916): Op. 49, Nos. 1 and 2 Sonatas (*U.E.*); Op. 107 Sonata (*Böte & Bock*)

REISSIGER, CARL (1798–1859): Op. 146 Fantasy (*Litolff*)

REITER, A.: Sonatine (*Döblinger*)

REVEL, P. (cont. French): Fantaisie (*Leduc*)

RHEINBERGER, J. G. (1839–1901): Op. 105a Sonata (*Kistner*)

RICHARDSON, ALAN (b. 1904): Roundelay (*O.U.P.*); Op. 22 Three Pieces (*Augener*)

RICKSTAL, JOS. VAN: Improvisation (*Alsbach*)

RIETHMULLER, HELMUT: Op. 36 Sonata (*Peters*)

ROCHAT, ANDREE: Tre Canzoni e Tre Intermezzi (*Carisch*)

ROCHBERG, G.: Dialogues (*U.E.*)

DE ROOS, ROBERT (b. 1907): Cappriccio (*Donemus*)

ROSSINI, G. (1792–1868): Fantaisie (*Schott*)

ROUSSEL, ALBERT (1869–1937): Aria (*Leduc*)

ROY, ALPHONSE: Serenade (*Richli*)

ROZSA, M. (b. 1907): Op. 27 Sonatine (unaccomp.) (*M.R.*)

RUEFF, J. (cont. French): Concertino (*Leduc*)

RUGGIERO, GIUSEPPE: Six Caprices (*Hinrichsen*)

RUNGIS, R. (cont. French): Seven Pieces (*Lemoine*)

RUYNEMAN, DANIEL (b. 1886): Sonata (*Donemus*)

RYTEL, P. (b. 1884): Op. 26 Romance (*Polish State Publishing House*)

SAINT-SAËNS, C. (1835–1921): Op. 167 Sonata (*Durand*)

SAMUEL, HAROLD (1879–1937): Three Light Pieces (*B. & H.*)

SAUVAGE, CAMILLE: Rhapsodie nostalgique (*Editions Imperia*)

SCHMID, E. (b. 1907): Rhapsody

SCHMID, HEINRICH K.: Op. 34, No. 2 Allegretto (*Schott*)

SCHMITT, FLORENT (1870–1958): Op. 30, No. 1 Andantino (*Leduc*)

SCHMUTZ, A. D.: Poème Rhapsodie (*Belwin*)

SCHOLLUM, R. (b. 1913): Op. 55 No. 4 Sonatine (*Döblinger*)

SCHOUWMAN, HANS (b. 1902): Op. 37 Aubade and Barcarolle (*Donemus*)

SCHUMANN, R. (1810–56): Op. 73 Phantasiestucke (*Chappell*)

SCONTRINO, ANTONIO (1850–1922): 6 Bozzetti (*Brizzi & Niccolai, Florence*)

SEARLE, HUMPHREY (b. 1915): Op. 32 Suite (*Schott*)

SEIBER, MÁTYÁS (1905–60): Andantino Pastorale (*Schott*)

SEROCKI, K.: Dance (*M.R.*)

SETACCIOLI, G. (1868–1925): Op. 31 Sonata (*Ricordi*)

SHAW, CHRISTOPHER (cont. British): Sonata (*Novello*)

SICCARDI, H. (b. 1897): Preludio y Fuga (*Ed Argentina de Musica*)

SIMON, A.: Concert Piece Op. 31 (*M.R.*)

SLONIMSKY, NICHOLAS (b. 1895): Four Russian Melodies (*Leeds Music Corp., U.S.A.*)

SOWERBY, L. (b. 1895): Sonata (*Schirmer*)

SPINNER, LEOPOLD: Op. 10 Suite (*B. & H.*)

SPOHR, L. (1784–1859): Op. 81 Fantasia and Variations (*Schmidt*); Three Adagios (*Augener*)

STANFORD, C. V. (1852–1924): Op. 129 Sonata (*S. & B.*); Op. 13 Three Intermezzi (*Novello*)

STAROKADOMSKY, M. (b. 1901): Five Pieces (*Leeds Music Corp., U.S.A.*)

STEENHUIS, FRANÇOIS: Sonatina (*Musikhandel Alberson*)

STEKKE, LEON: Andante Appassionata (*Editions Brogneaux, Brussels*)

STEVENS, HALSEY: Suite (*Hinrichsen*)

STRAVINSKY, I. (b. 1882): Trois Pièces (unaccomp.) (*Chester*)

STRIMER (cont. French): Pastorale Caucasienne (*Durand*)

SUTERMEISTER, H. (b. 1910): Capriccio (unaccomp.) (*Schott*)

SWAIN, FREDA (b. 1902): The Willow Tree (*British & Continental*); Rhapsody (*MS.*); Two Contrasts (*Joseph Williams*)

SZALOWSKI, A. (b. 1923): Sonatina (*Omega*)

TANEIEV, S. (1856–1915): Canzona (*U.S.S.R. State Music*); Arabesque (*Andrieu*); Sonata (*M.R.*)

TEMPLETON, ALEC (b. 1909): Pocket-sized Sonata (*Leeds Music Corp., U.S.A.*)

TOMASI, H. (b. 1901): Pieces include: Introduction et Danse (*Leduc*)

TOVEY, D. (1875–1940): Op. 16 Sonata (*Schott*)

TUTHILL, B. C.: Op. 3 Fantasy Sonata, 1936 (*Fischer*)

VASSILENKO, S. (b. 1872): Op. 47 Oriental Dance (*U.S.S.R. State Music*)

VAUGHAN, WILLIAMS, R. (1872–1958): Six Studies in English Folk Song (*S. & B.*)

VITO DELVAUX, B.: Divertissement (*Brogneaux*)

VLADIGUEROV, P.: Aquarelles (*M.R.*)

VLAG, HARREND: Ballade (*Ed Heuwekemeye, Amsterdam*)

VOGEL, J. (b. 1894): Sonatina (*M.R.*)

WALKER, ERNEST (1870–1949): Op. 9 Romance (*Joseph Williams*)

WALTER, F.: Two Fantasy Pieces (*Novello*)

WALTHEW, R. (1872–1951): Pieces include Suite in F (*B. & H.*)

WANHAL, J. (1739–1813): Sonata in B flat (*Hinrichsen*)

WEBBER, LLOYD (cont. British): Theme and Variations, 1952 (*Francis, Day, & Hunter*)

WEBER, C. M. (1786–1826): Op. 47 Grand Duo Concertante (*B. & H.*); Op. 33 Theme and Variations (*Schlesinger*)

WEINBERGER, J. (b. 1896): Sonatine (*Fischer*)

WEINER, L. (b. 1885): Op. 8 Ballade (*Rózsavölgyi*); Op. 40 Peregi Verbunk (Czardas) (*M.R.*)

WEIS, FLEMING (b. 1898): Sonata (*Kistner*)

WEISMANN (1879–1950): Op. 72 Sonata (*Richard Birnbach*)

WELLESZ, EGON (b. 1885): Op. 34 Two Pieces (*U.E.*)

WIDOR, C. M. (1845–1937): Op. 72 Introduction et Rondo (*Heugel*)

WILDGANS, F. (b. 1913): Op. 14 Three Pieces (*U.E.*)

WILSON, T.: Sonatina (*Schott*)

WIRTH, H.: Sonata (*M.R.*)

WORDSWORTH, WILLIAM (b. 1908): Prelude and Scherzo (*Lengnick*)

YUILLE-SMITH, C. R.: Op. 3, No. 2 Gavotte (*O.U.P.*)

ZVEREV: Three Lyrical Pieces (*U.S.S.R. State Music*)

CONCERTOS
(with full orchestra unless otherwise stated)

ANDRÉ, PAUL (cont. French): Concertino for 2 cl. (*Deplaix*)

ARNOLD, MALCOLM (b. 1921): Concerto with str. orch. (*Lengnick*)

BAUTISTA, JULIAN (b. 1901): Fantasia Española (*MS., U.E.*)

BEN HAIM, P. (cont. Palestinian): Pastorale Variée, str. orch. & hp. (*Chester*)

BENTZON, JØRGEN (1897–1948): Chamber Concerto with small orch. (*Dania, Copenhagen*)

BEREZOVSKY, N. T. (b. 1900): Op. 28 Concerto (*B. & H.*)

BERNAUD: Concerto Lyrique (*U.M.P.*)

BINET, JEAN (b. 1893): Petit Concert with str. orch. (*Edition Henn, Geneva*)

BJELINSKI, BRUNO: Concerto with str. orch. (*Zagreb Academy*)

BONSEL, A. (cont. Dutch): Concerto with str. orch. & cel., 2 hp., perc. (*Donemus*)

BOZZA, EUGENE (cont. French): Concerto with chamber orch. (*Leduc*)

BRUCH, MAX (1838–1920): Concerto for cl., vla., & orch. (*Eichmann*)

BRUNS, V.: Concerto (*Hofmeister*)

BUSONI, FERRUCCIO (1866–1924): Concertino (*Br. & H.*)

CASANOVA, ANDRÉ: Ballade for cl. & orch. (*Ricordi*)

COOKE, ARNOLD (b. 1906): Concerto with str. orch. (*Novello*)

COPLAND, AARON (b. 1900): Concerto with str. orch. & hp. (*B. & H.*)

CRUFT, ADRIAN (b. 1921): Concertino with str. orch. (*Joseph Williams*)

CRUSELL, B. (1775–1838): Op. 5 Concerto (*M.R.*)

DABELEYEV, B.: Concerto (*M.R.*)

DEBUSSY, CLAUDE (1862–1918): Première Rhapsodie (*Durand*)

DELLO JOIO, N. (b. 1913): Concertante (*M.R.*)

DORBRZYNSKI, I. F.: Concerto (*Polish State Publishing House*)

DRESDEN, SEM (b. 1881): Sinfonietta (*De Wolfe*)

ECKHARDT-GRAMMATTÉ, S. (b. 1902): Triple Concerto for trpt., cl., bn., & orch. (*U.E.*)

EVANS, PETER (b. 1929): Concerto with str. orch. (*MS.*)

FINZI, GERALD (b. 1901): Concerto with str. orch. (*B. & H.*)

FLOTHIUS, MARIUS (b. 1914): Op. 58 Concerto with str. orch., hp., perc. (*Donemus*); Sinfonietta concertante for cl., alto sax. & small orch. (*Donemus*)

GABLER, EGON (nineteenth century): Two Concertos (*Oertel, Hanover*)

GALLON, NOEL (cont. French): Concerto for ob., cl., bn. (*Leduc*)

GODRON, HUGO (cont. Dutch): Concerto with str. orch. (*Donemus*); Amabile Suite for cl., pf., str. orch. (*Donemus*)

GOLDSCHMIDT, B.: Concerto (*MS.*)

HAMILTON, IAIN (b. 1922): Op. 7 Concerto (*MS., Schott*)

HINDEMITH, PAUL (b. 1895): Concerto (*Schott*); Quadruple Concerto for fl., cor ang., cl., bn. (*Schott*); Concerto for cl., trpt. with str. orch. (*M.R.*)

HODDINOTT, ALUN (b. 1929): Concerto with str. orch. (*O.U.P.*)

HODGSON, PETER (cont. British): Concert Piece (*Hinrichsen*); Concerto with str. orch. (*Hinrichsen*)

HOLBROOKE, J. (b. 1878): Quadruple Concerto for fl., ob., cl., & bn. (*De Wolfe*)

HOROVITZ, J. (b. 1926): Concertante with str. orch., 1953 (*Chester*); Op. 7 Concerto with str. orch. (*Mills*)

JELLINEK, H. (b. 1901): Op. 18 Phantasie for cl., pf., & orch. (*U.E.*)

JETTEL, RUDY (cont. Austrian): Introduction and Variations on an original theme (*Kliment*)

JONGEN, JOS (1873–1953): Concertino (*Gervan*)

KEYS, I. (b. 1919): Concerto with str. orch. (*Novello*)

KOPPEL, H. D. (b. 1908): Op. 35 Concerto (*Skandinavisk*)

KROMMER, F. V. (1759–1831): Op. 36 Concerto (*Artia, B. & H.*)

KRYUKOV, V.: Op. 56 Concertino (*M.R.*)

KUBÍN, RUDOLF (b. 1909): Concerto (*Kudelik*)

KURPINSKI, K.: Concerto (*Polish State Publishing House*)

LANDRÉ, GUILLAUME (b. 1905): 4 Miniatures cl. and str. orch. (without db.) (*Donemus*)

MACDONALD, MALCOLM (cont. British): Concerto with str. orch. (*MS.*); Cuban Rondo (*Ricordi*)

MACONCHY, ELIZABETH (b. 1907): Concertino with str. orch. (*MS.*)

MALKO, N.: Concerto (*B. & H.*)

MANEVICH, A.: Concerto (1955) (*M.R.*)

MANN, J. G. H.: Op. 90 Concerto (*Ruhle & Wendling*)

MILHAUD, DARIUS (b. 1892): Concerto (*Elkan Vogel*); Scaramouche, Suite in 3 parts (*Salabert*)

MOZART, W. A. (1756–91): K. 622 Concerto; K. 297*b* Sinfonia Concertante for ob., cl., bn., hn.

NIELSEN, CARL (1865–1931): Op. 57 Concerto (*Dania*)

NORDEN, HUGO: Concertino in G (*Arthur Schmidt, Mass.*)

NYSTEDT: Concertino for cl., cor ang. with str. orch. (*Hinrichsen*)

PAULSON, J.: Concertos No. 1 & 2 (*M.R.*)

PITT, P. (1870–1932): Op. 22 Concertino (*B. & H.*)

POKORNY, FRANZ (1729–70): Concerto in E flat (*Br. & H.*); Concerto in B flat (*Br. & H.*)

RAWSTHORNE, ALAN (b. 1905): Concerto with str. orch. (*MS., O.U.P.*)

REISSIGER, C. G. (1798–1859): Op. 63 Concertino (*Schmidt*)

RIETZ, J. (1812–77): Op. 29 Concerto (*Kistner*)

RIMSKY-KORSAKOV, N. (1844–1908): Concerto with military band (*B. & H.*)

RIVIER, JEAN (b. 1896): Concerto with str. orch. (*U.M.P.*)

ROSETTI, F. A. (1746–92): Concerto à Clarinette principalle (*Sieber*)

SAINT-SAËNS, C. (1835–1921): Op. 6 Tarantelle for fl., cl., & orch. (*Leduc*)

SCHIBLER, ARMIN (b. 1920): Op. 49 Concertino (*Eulenburg*)

SCHOLLUM, ROBERT (b. 1913): Werk 34 Concerto grosso with small orch. (*U.E.*)

SCHOUWMAN, HANS (b. 1902): 5 Sketches with small orch. (*Donemus*)

SEIBER, MÁTYÁS (1905–60): Concertino with str. orch. (*Schott*)

SIKORSKI, K.: Concerto (*Polish State Publishing House*)

SPAIN-DUNK, SUSAN (cont. British): Cantilena (*Elkin*)

SPOHR, L. (1784–1859): Four Concertos: Op. 26 No. 1 (*Hinrichsen*); Op. 57 No. 2 (*Peters*); Nos. 3 & 4 (*Br. & H.*)

STAMITZ, JOHANN (1717–57): Concerto with str. orch. (*Leeds Music Corp., U.S.A.*)

STAMITZ, KARL (1745–1801): Concerto in E flat (*Sikorski*); Duo concerto for cl. & bn. (*Sikorski*)

STANFORD, CHARLES (1852–1924): Op. 80 Concerto (*MS., S. & B.*)

STOLZENBERG, GEORG (nineteenth–twentieth century): Op. 6 Serenade with str. orch. (*Br. & H.*)

STRATEGIER, H. (b. 1912): Concertino (*Donemus*)

STRAUSS, RICHARD (1864–1949): Duet-Concertino for cl. & bn. with str. orch. & hp. (*B. & H.*)

STRAVINSKY, I. (b. 1882): Ebony Concerto with military band (*Chappell*)

SVERVANSKY, E.: Serenade with str. orch. (*M.R.*)

TOMASI, M. (b. 1901): Concerto (*Leduc*)

TUTHILL, B.: Op. 28 Concerto (*Elkan Vogel*)

UHL, ALFRED (b. 1909): Konzertante Sinfonie (*U.E.*)

VASILENKO, S. (b. 1872): Op. 135 Concerto (*M.R.*)

VEALE, JOHN (b. 1922): Concerto (*O.U.P.*)

VILLA-LOBOS, H. (1887–1959): Chorus No. 3, 'Pica-Pao' for cl., sax., bn., 2 hn., tromb. (men's chorus *ad lib.*) (*Schott*)

VINTER, GILBERT (cont. British): Concertino (*B. & H.*)

VOORMOLEN, ALEXANDER (b. 1895): Sinfonia concertante for cl., hn., & str. orch. (*Donemus*)

WEBER, C. M. (1786–1826): Op. 26 Concertino; Op. 73 Concerto in F minor; Op. 74 Concerto in E flat

WHETTAM, GRAHAM (cont. British): Serenade No. 1 (*De Wolfe*)

WILDGANS, FRIEDRICH (b. 1913): Second Concerto with small orch. (*U.E.*)

CLARINET & OTHER WIND INSTRUMENTS
(with or without piano and double bass)

Wind quintet (unless otherwise stated) is fl., ob., cl., bn., hn.

ABRAMSKY, A. (b. 1898): Concertino for fl., cl., hn., bn., pf., 1929 (*U.E.*)

ADDISON, JOHN (b. 1920): Trio for ob., cl., bn. (*Joseph Williams*); Sextet for fl., ob., cor ang., cl., bcl., bn. (*MS.*); Serenade for wind quint. & hp. (*O.U.P.*)

AGAY, D. : Five Easy Dances for wind quint. (*U.E.*)

ALPAERTS, FLOR (b. 1876): Evening Music for 2 fl., 2 ob., 2 cl., 2 bn. (*Metropolis*)

AMBERG, J. (b. 1846): Suite for fl., ob., cl., pf. (*Hansen*)

ANDRIESSEN, JURIAAN (b. 1925): Octet for fl., 2 ob., 2 cl., bcl., 2 bn. (*Donemus*); 'L'incontro de Cesar'e Cleopatra' for wind quint. & pf. (*Donemus*)

APIVOR, DENNIS (b. 1916): Concertante for cl., pf., 2 perc. (*MS.*)

APOSTEL, H. E. (b. 1901): Op. 14 Quartet for fl., cl., hn., bn. (*U.E.*); Op. 20 Five Bagatelles for fl., cl., bn. (*U.E.*)

ARNELL, RICHARD (b. 1917): Cassation for wind quint. (*Hinrichsen*); Serenade for double wind quint. & contra bn. (or db.) (*Hinrichsen*)

ARNOLD, MALCOLM (b. 1921): Op. 37 Divertimento for fl., ob., cl. (*Paterson*); Sea Shanties for wind quint. (*Paterson*)

ARRIEU, C. (b. 1903): Trio for ob., cl., bn. (*Amphion*)

AURIC, G. (b. 1899): Trio for ob., cl., bn. (*Oiseau Lyre*)

BAAREN, KEES VAN: Trio for fl., cl., bn. (*Ed. Parrhysius*); Trio for fl., cl., bn. (*Donemus*)

BACH, C. P. E. (1714–88): Six Marches for 2 ob., 2 cl., 2 hn., 2 bn.; Six Sonatas for cl., bn., pf. (*International*)

BADINGS, HENK (b. 1907): 3 Netherlands Dances for hn., 2 trpt., tromb. (*Tierolff*); Two Wind Quintets (*Donemus*); Trio for ob., cl., bn. (*Donemus*); Sextet for wind quint. & pf. (*Donemus*)

BAKALEINIKOV, V.: Introduction and Scherzo for wind quint. (*Belwin*)

BALAY (cont. French): Three wind quintets (*Leduc*)

BALBO: Three Etchings for fl. (or ob.) & cl. (*Chester*)

BARBER, S. (b. 1910): Op. 31 Summer Music for wind quint. (*Schirmer*)

BARRAUD, H. (b. 1900): Trio for ob., cl., bn. (*Oiseau Lyre*)

BARROW, J. R.: March for wind quint. (*Schirmer*)

BARTHE, A.: Passacaille for wind quint. (*Leduc*)

BARTOS, FR. (b. 1905): Suite, Le Bourgeois, for wind quint.

BAUER, MARION (b. 1897): Prelude, Improvisation, Pastorale, Dance for cl. and ob. (*Hinrichsen*)

BAUERNFEIND, H.: Heitere Musik for ob., cl., bn. (*Döblinger*)

BAVICCHI, JOHN: Six duets for fl., cl. (*O.U.P.*)

BEEKHUIS, HANNA: Elegie en humoresque for wind quint. (*Donemus*)

BEETHOVEN, L. VAN (1770–1827): Three Duos for cl. and bn.; Op. 16 Quintet for ob., cl., hn., bn., pf.; Op. 71 Sextet for 2 cl., 2 bn., 2 hn.; Op. 103 Octet for 2 ob., 2 cl., 2 hn., 2 bn.; Op. 146 Rondino for 2 ob., 2 cl., 2 hn., 2 bn.

BENTZON, J. (1897–1948): Op. 7 Sonatine for fl., cl., bn. (*Skandinavisk*); Op. 31 Racconto No. 3 for ob., cl., bn. (*Skandinavisk*); Racconto No. 5 for wind quint. (*Skandinavisk*)

BEREZOVSKY, N. T. (b. 1900): Op. 11 Suite for fl., ob., cl., cor ang., bn. (*Ed. Russe*)

BERGER, A. (b. 1912): Duo for ob. & cl. (*Hindrichsen*)

BERGSMA, WILLIAM: Quartet in C major for fl., ob., cl., bn. (*U.S.*)

BERNARD, E.: Op. 36 Divertissement for 2 fl., 2 ob., 2 cl., 2 hn., 2 bn. (*Durand*)

BIERSACK, A.: Divertimento for fl., cl., bn., 1908 (*Schott*)

BIRTWISTLE, HARRISON (b. 1934): Refrains & Choruses for wind quint. (*U.E.*); 'The World is Discovered' for double wind quint., guitar, hp. (*U.E.*); Sonatina for wind quint. (*U.E.*)

BITSCH (cont. French): Divertissement for fl., ob., cl. (*Leduc*)

BLACHER, BORIS (b. 1903): Op. 38 Divertimento for fl., ob., cl., bn., 1952 (*Schott*)

BLOCH, E. (1880–1959): Concertino for fl., cl., pf. (*Schirmer*)

BLOCK, F.: Sonatina for 2 cl. (*Levant Music Corp.*)

BLUMER, T. (b. 1882): Op. 52 Wind quintet. (*Zimmermann*); Op. 53 Suite for fl., ob., cl., bn. (*Simrock*); Op. 45 Sextet for wind quint. and pf. (*Simrock*)

BOËLLMAN, L. (1862–97): Menuet Gothique for ob., cor ang., cl., bn., hn. (*Durand*)

BOISDEFFRE, R. DE (1838–1906): Op. 49 Sextet for fl., ob., cl., bn., hn., pf. (*Hamelle*)

BONFIL, J. S.: 3 Grands Duos for 2 cl., 1810 (*Decombe*)

BONNEAU, P. (cont. French): 3 Noëls Anciens for ob., cl., bn. (*Leduc*)

BONSEL, ADRIAN (cont. Dutch): Two wind quintets (*De Wolfe*)

BORKOVEC, P.: Wind quintet (*M.R.*)

BORRIS, S.: Terzettino for fl., cl., bn. (*Sirius*); Octet for fl., ob., cl., bcl., bn., 2 hn., trpt. (*Sirius*); Op. 25, No. 2 Wind quintet (*Sirius*)

BOUFFIL, J.: Op. 7 & 8 Trios for 3 cl. (*Cundy-Bettoney*)

BOUTRY: Divertissement for ob., cl., bn. (*U.M.P.*)

O'BOVE, J. H.: Petit Trio for fl. (or ob.), cl., bn. (*Fischer*)

BOWEN, YORK (1884–1961): Miniature Suite for fl., ob., 2 cl., bn. (*De Wolfe*)

BOWLES, P. (b. 1911): Music for a farce for cl., trpt., perc., pf. (*U.S.*)

BOYAN, G.: Trio for ob., cl., bn. (*M.R.*)

BOZZA, E. (cont. French): Suite brève for ob., cl., bn. (*Leduc*); Op. 42 Variations sur un thème libre for wind quint. (*Leduc*); Op. 48 Scherzo for wind quint. (*Leduc*); Trois Pièces pour une musique de nuit for fl., ob., cl., bn. (*Leduc*)

BRERO, CESARE: Trio for fl., cl., bn. (*Ricordi*)

BRIDGE, FRANK (1879–1941): Divertimento for fl., ob., cl., bn. (*B. & H.*)

BRUNS, V.: Wind quintet (*Hofmeister*)

BURIAN, E. F.: Wind quintet (*M.R.*)

BURKHARD, W. (b. 1900): Serenade for fl., cl. (*U.E.*)

BURT, FRANCIS: Trio for fl., cl., bn. (*MS.*)

BUTTERWORTH, ARTHUR (cont. British): Trio for ob., cl., bn. (*Hinrichson*)

CAILLIET (cont. French): Overture in B flat for wind quint. (*Elkan Vogel*)

CAMERA, J.: Suite for fl., cl., bn. (*M.R.*)

CANTELOUBE: Suite Rustique for wind quint. (*U.M.P.*)

CARTAN, J. (1906–32): Sonatine for fl., cl. (*Heugel*)

CARTER, ELLIOTT (b. 1908): Wind quintet (*Schott*); Eight Etudes & a Fantasy for fl., ob., cl., bn. (*Schott*)

CARWITHEN, DOREEN (cont. British): Wind quintet (*MS.*)

CASTÉRÈDE: Wind quintet (*U.M.P.*)

CAZDEN: Three Constructions for wind quint. (*Kalmus*)

CETTIER, P. (b. 1874): Quintet for fl., ob., cl., bn., pf. (*Senart*)

CHAGRIN, FRANCIS (b. 1905): Divertimento for wind quint. (*Augener*)

CHAILLEY, J. (b. 1910): Barcarolle for wind quint. (*Leduc*)

CHAVEZ, CARLOS (b. 1899): Soli for ob., cl., trpt., bn. (*B. & H.*)

CHAYNES: Serenade for wind quint. (*U.M.P.*)

CHEMIN-PETIT, H. (1864–1917): Trio in Olden Style for ob., cl., bn. (*Hinrichsen*); Wind quintet (*Hinrichsen*)

CHWARTZ, L.: Evening in the Turkestan Steppes for fl., cor ang. (ob.), cl., bn. (*B. & H.*)

CLEMENTI, ALDO: Tre piccoli pezzi for fl., ob., cl. (*Suvini Zerboni*)

CLIQUET-PLEYEL, H.: Chant d'Esperance for cl., bn., pf. (*Editions Sociales Internationales, Paris*)

COLACO, OSORIO-SWAAB: Suite for wind quint. (*Donemus*)

COLE, HUGO (cont. British): Trio for pf., fl., cl. (*Novello*)

COLOMER (cont. French): Bourrée for wind quint. (*Leduc*)

CONSTANT, MARIUS (cont. French): Trio for ob., cl., bn. (*Chester*)

COOKE, ARNOLD (b. 1906): Suite for three clarinets (*O.U.P.*)

COWELL, H. (b. 1897): Suite for wind quint.

COX, NOEL: Minuet for fl., ob., cl., bn. (*B. & H.*)

CRUSELL, B. (1775–1838): 3 Duos d'une difficulté progressive, for 2 cl. (*Peters*)

DAHLHOFF, W.: Der Choral von Leuthen for wind quint. (*Schmidt*); Drei Sätze for fl., ob., cl. (*Schmidt*); Forest Secrets for fl., ob., 2 cl., bn. (*Schmidt*); A Dramatic Dance Scene for fl., ob., cl., bn. (*Schmidt*)

DAMASE, J. M. (b. 1928): 17 Variations for wind quint. (*Leduc*)

DANIEL, LESUR (b. 1908): Suite for ob., cl., bn. (*M.R.*)

DANZI, F. (1763–1826): Op. 67 Various wind quintets including Quintet No. 2 in E minor (*Hinrichsen*)

DAVID, GYULA: Serenade for wind quint. (*Mills*)

DAVID, J. N. (b. 1895): Divertimento for wind quint., pf. (*Br. & H.*)

DAVIES, PETER MAXWELL (b. 1934): Alma Redemptoris Mater for fl., ob., 2 cl., hn., bn. (*Schott*)

DEMUTH, NORMAN (b. 1898): Pastorale and Scherzo for wind quint. (*Hinrichsen*)

DESORMIÈRE, R. (b. 1905): 6 Danceries du XVIème Siècle for fl., cl., cor ang., bn., hn. (*Durand*)

DESTENAY, E. (cont. French): Op. 27 Trio for ob., cl., pf. (*Leduc*)

DEVIENNE, F.: Overture for 2 fl., 2 ob., 2 cl. (*Hofmeister*)

DIJK, JAN VAN: Duo for cl., bn. (*Donemus*)

DITTERSDORF, K. D. VON (1739–99): Divertimento in B flat for 2 ob., 2 cl., 2 bn. (*Sikorski*)

DOBRZYNSKI: Duet for cl., hn. (*Polish State Publishing House*)

DOMANSKY, A.: Divertimento for 2 cl., hn., bn. (*Schmidt*); Wind quintet (*Schmidt*); Quintet for fl., 2 cl., hn., bn. (*Schmidt*)

DOMENICO, OLIVIO DI: Wind quintet (*U.M.P.*)

DONATO, A.: Three Pieces for 3 cl. (*U.E.*)

DONOVAN, R. (b. 1891): Wind quintet

DOST, R. (b. 1877): Septet for wind quint., pf., perc. (*Zimmermann*)

DOUGLAS, ROY (b. 1907): 6 Dance Caricatures for fl., ob., cl. (*Hinrichsen*)

DRESDEN, SEM (b. 1881): Suite (after Rameau) for wind quint., pf. (*Donemus*); Third Suite for pf., fl. (picc.), ob. (cor ang.), cl., bn., hn. (*Donemus*); Petite Suite for fl., ob. (cor ang.), cl., bn., hn., pf. (*Donemus*)

DUBOIS, T. (1837–1924): Suites 1 & 2 for 2 fl., ob., 2 cl., hn., 2 bn. (*Leduc*); Dixtuor for 2 fl., 2 ob., 2 cl., 2 hn., 2 bn. (*U.M.P.*)

DUBOIS, P. M.: Fantasia for wind quint. (*U.M.P.*)

DUNCAN, E. (1886–1920): Op. 38 Quintet for fl., cl., hn., bn., pf. (*B. & H.*)

EDER, H.: Op. 25 Wind quintet (*Döblinger*)

EISENMANN, W.: Divertimento for 2 cl., bn.

ELTON, A.: Short Sonata for 2 cl. (*Chester*)

EMMANUEL, M.: Trio-Sonate for cl., fl., pf. (*Lemoine*)

ENESCO, GEORGES (1881–1955): Dixtuor for double wind quint. (*Enoch*)

ESCHER, RUDOLF (b. 1912): Trio for ob., cl., bn. (*Donemus*)

ESSEX, KENNETH: Wind quintet (*Hinrichsen*)

ETLER, A.: Wind quintet (*Schott*)

FELDERHOF, JAN: Theme & Variations for ob., cl., bn. (*Donemus*)

FELLEGARA, VITTORIO: Octet for fl., ob., cl., bn., hn., 2 trpt., tromb. (*Suvini Zerboni*))

FERNANDEZ, O.: Three Inventions for cl., bn. (*M.R.*)

FERROUD, P. O. (1900–35): Trio in E for ob., cl., bn. (*Durand*)

FITELBERG, J. (b. 1879): Capriccio for fl., ob., cl., bcl., tromb. (or bn.) (*Omega*)

FLÈGIER, A. (1846–1927): Trio for ob., cl., bn. (*Gallet*)

FLOTHUIS, M. (b. 1914): Op. 11 Nocturne for fl., ob., cl. (*Chester*); Op. 13 Quintet for fl., ob., cl., bcl., bn. (*Donemus*)

FOERSTER, J. B. (1859–1951): Op. 95 Wind quintet (*Hudebni*); Sextet for pf., wind quint. (*Hudebni*)

FORET, FELICIEN (cont. French): Suite en Trio for ob., cl., bn. (*Costallat*)

FORTNER, WOLFGANG (b. 1907): Five Bagatelles for wind quint. (*Schott*)

FRANÇAIX, JEAN (b. 1912): Divertissement for ob., cl., bn. (*Schott*); Wind quintet (*Schott*); Quartet for fl., ob., cl., bn. (*Schott*)

FRANK, ALAN (b. 1910): Suite for 2 cl. (*O.U.P.*)

FRENSEL WEGENER, E.: Sextet for wind quint., pf. (*Donemus*)

FRICKER, PETER RACINE (b. 1920): Wind quintet (*Schott*)

FRID, GÉZA (b. 1904): Serenade for fl., 2 cl., bn., hn. (*Donemus*)

FROMMEL, GERHARD: Concertino for tenor hn. (or tromb.) & fl., ob., 2 cl., bn., hn. (*Schott*)

FUHRMEISTER, F. (b. 1862): Gavotte and Tarantella for pf. & wind quint. (*Zimmermann*)

FURST, P. W.: Konzertante Musik for wind quint. (*U.E.*)

FUSSEN, W.: Wind quintet (*M.R.*)

GABAYE: Wind quintet (*U.M.P.*)

GABRIEL, M. (1825–77): Dans la calme nuit for ob., cl., pf. (*Lemoine*)

GAL, H. (b. 1890): Divertimento (1925) for fl., ob., 2 cl., 2 hn., 2 bn. (*Leukart*)

GEBAUER, F. R. (1775–1844): Sechs Konzertante Duos for 2 cl. Also for cl. & bn. (*Sikorsky*)

GENARRO, M. (twentieth century): Trio for fl., ob., cl. (*Leduc*)

GENIN (late nineteenth century): Duo Concertante for fl., cl., pf. (*Costallat*); Sextet for wind quint. & pf. (*Eschig*)

GENTILHOMME: Wind quintet (*Hudebni*)

GENZMER, HARALD (b. 1909): Wind quintet (*Hinrichsen*)

GERAEDTS, JAAP: Divertimento No. 1 for ob., cl., bn. (*Donemus*); Divertimento No. 2 for ob., cl., bn. (*Donemus*)

GERDELER, D.: Quartet for fl., ob., cl., bn. (*M.R.*)

GERHARD, ROBERTO (b. 1896): Wind quintet (*Hinrichsen*)

GERSTER, O. (b. 1897): Wind quintet (*Schott*); Heitere Musik for wind quint. (*Schott*)

GIESEKING, WALTER (1895–1956): Quintet for ob., cl., hn., bn., pf. (*B. & H.*)

GIPPS, RUTH (b. 1921): Trio for ob., cl., pf. (*MS.*); Seascape for double wind quint. (*Sam Fox*)

GLINKA, M. I. (1804–57): Trio Pathétique for cl., bn., pf. (*Jurgenson*)

GODRON, HUGO: Serenade for wind quint. & pf. (*Donemus*)

GOEB, ROGER (b. 1914): Suite for woodwind trio for ob., cl., bn. (*U.S.*)

GOEPFART, K. E. (1859–1942): Quartet for fl., cl., bn., pf.

GOEPFERT, C. A.: Six Duos Faciles for cl., bn. (*Hofmeister*)

GOLESTAN, STAN (b. 1875): Petite Suite Bucolique en forme de Trio for ob., cl., bn. (*Durand*)

GOOSSENS, EUGENE (b. 1893): Op. 40 Phantasy-Nonet for fl., ob., 2 cl., 2 bn., 2 hn., trpt. (*Curwen*)

GOUNOD, C. (1818–93): Petite Symphonie for fl., 2 ob., 2 cl., 2 hn., 2 bn. (*Costallat*)

GOUVY, L. T. (1819–98): Op. 71 Octet for fl., ob., 2 cl., 2 hn., 2 bn. (*Kistner*); Op. 90 Petite Suite Gauloise for fl., 2 ob., 2 cl., 2 hn., 2 bn. (*U.E.*)

GRAINGER, PERCY (b. 1882): Walking Tune for wind quint. (*Schott*)

GRUNENWALD (cont. French): Fantaisie Arabesque for ob., cl., bn., pf. (*Salabert*)

HAAN, STEFAN DE (cont. British): Divertimento for cl. & bn. (*Hinrichsen*); Trio for ob., cl., bn. (*Hinrichsen*)

HANDEL (ed. K. Haas) (1685–1759): Overture for 2 cl. and hn. (*Schott*)

D'HARCOURT: Rhapsodie Peruvienne for ob., cl., bn. (*U.M.P.*)

HARDING, K. (cont. British): Quartet for 3 cl., bcl. (*MS.*)

HARTMANN, E. (1836–98): Serenade for fl., ob., 2 cl., 2 hn., 2 bn. (*Ries & Erler*)

HAYDN, J. (1732–1809): Octet for 2 ob., 2 cl., 2 hn., 2 bn. (*International Music Co.*)

F

HAYDN, J. (contd.): Divertimento for 2 cl., 2 hn. (*Hansen*)

HEIM, M.: Wind Quintet (*Schmidt*)

HENKEMANS, HANS (b. 1913): Wind quintet (*Donemus*)

HENNESSY, SWAN (b. 1886): Trio for 2 cl., bn. (*Demets*)

HENZE, H. W. (b. 1926): Wind quintet (*Schott*)

HERMANS, NICO: Op. 2 Divertimento piccolo for ob., cl., bn. (*Donemus*)

HERZOGENBERG, H. VON (1843–1900): Op. 43 Quintet for ob., cl., hn., bn., pf. (*Peters*)

HESS, W.: 5 Duos for 2 cl. in form of a Suite (*Hinrichsen*); Op. 51 Divertimento for wind quint. (*Hinrichsen*)

HILL, E. B. (b. 1872): Op. 39 Sextet for wind quint. & pf. (*Schirmer*)

HINDEMITH, PAUL (b. 1895): Op. 24, No. 2 Kleine Kammermusik for wind quint. (*Schott*); Septet for fl., ob., cl., bcl., bn., hn., trpt. (*Schott*)

HOFFDING, F. (b. 1899): Wind quintet (*Skandinavisk*); Dialoger for ob., cl. (*Skandinavisk*)

HÖFFER, PAUL (1895–1949): Theme and Variations for ob., cl., bn. (*M.R.*); Wind quintet (*M.R.*); Little Suite for ob., cl., bn. (*M.R.*)

HOLBROOKE, J. (b. 1878): Serenade for fl., ob., cl., bn.; Miniature Characteristic Suite for wind quint. (*De Wolfe*); Op. 33*a* Sextet for wind quint., pf. (*Chester*)

HOLMBOE, V. (b. 1909) Wind quintet (*M.R.*)

HONEGGER, A. (1892–1955): Rhapsody for 2 fl., cl., pf. (*Salabert*)

HOYER, K. (1891–1936): Serenade for wind quint. (*Chester*)

HUBER, H. (1852–1921): Op. 136 Quintet for fl., cl., hn., bn., pf. (*Hug*)

HUBER, KLAUS (b. 1924): Wind quintet (*MS.*)

HUGUES, L. (1836–1907): Op. 72 and 76 Quartets for fl., ob., cl., bn. (*Ricordi*); Allegro Scherzoso for 2 fl., ob., cl., bn. (*Ricordi*)

HURLSTONE, W. (1876–1906): Trio for cl., bn., pf. (*MS.*)

IBERT, J. (b. 1890): Cinq Pièces en Trio for ob., cl., bn. (*Oiseau Lyre*); Deux Mouvements for 2 fl., cl., bn. (*Leduc*); Trois Pièces Brèves for wind quint. (*Leduc*)

IKONOMOV, B.: Trio in E for ob., cl., bn. (*Oiseau Lyre*)

D'INDY, V. (1851–1931): Chansons et Danses for fl., ob., 2 cl., hn., 2 bn. (*Durand*); Op. 24 bis Sarabande et Menuet for wind quint. & pf. (*Hamelle*)

INGENHOVEN, J. (b. 1876): Wind quintet (*Wunderhorn-Verlag*)

INGRAM, HAROLD (b. 1904): Rhapsody for fl., cl., hp. (*MS.*); Fantasy for fl., ob., cl., hp., str. qt., db. (*MS.*)

IPPOLITOV-IVANOV (1859–1935): Evening in Georgia for fl., ob., cl., bn., hp. (or pf.) (*U.S.S.R. State Music*)

JACOB, GORDON (b. 1895): Wind quintet (*B. & H.*); Serenade for 2 fl., 2 ob., 2 cl., 2 bn. (*B. & H.*); Sextet for wind quint. & pf. (*M.R.*)

JACOBI, F. (b. 1891): Scherzo for wind quint. (*U.S.*)

JACOBSOHN, GABRIEL: Adagio and Allegro for cl., hn., bn. (*Israeli*)

JACOBSON, M. (b. 1896): Suite of Four Pieces for fl., cl., pf. (*Augener*)

JANÁČEK, L. (1854–1928): Suite, Mládí, for fl. (picc.), ob., cl., hn., bn., bcl. (*Hudebni*)

JARSILD, J.: Serenade 'Music making in Forest' for wind quint. (*Novello*)

JELLINEK, H. (b. 1913): Op. 9, No. 3 Six Aphorisms for 2 cl., bn. (*U.E.*); Op. 15, No. 8 Divertimento (Twelve-note Music) for E flat cl., B flat cl., basset-horn and bcl. (*U.E.*)

JEMNITZ, A. (b. 1890): Op. 20 Trio for fl., ob., cl. (*Zimmermann*)

JETTEL, R. (cont. Austrian): Sextet for fl., ob., 2 cl., hn., bn. (*Rubato-Verlag*)

JONES, DANIEL (b. 1912): Septet for fl., ob., cl., bcl., bn., hn., trpt. (*MS.*)

JONES, KENNETH V. (cont. British): Two wind quintets (*MS.*)

JONGEN, J. (1873–1953): Rhapsody for wind quint., pf. (*Chester*)

JONGEN, LEON (b. 1884): Trio for ob., cl., bn. (*Andraud*)

JOSEPHS, WILFRED (b. 1927): Five Fictitious Folk Songs for fl., ob., cl., bn. (*New Wind Music*)

JOSTEN, W. (b. 1885): Trio for fl., cl., bn. (*U.S.*)

JUON, PAUL (1872–1940): Divertimento for wind quint., pf. (*Schlesinger*); Op. 84 Wind quintet (*Lienau*); Op. 73 Arabesken for ob., cl., bn. (*Lienau*)

KALABIS, VIKTOR: Divertimento for wind quint. (*Czech State Publishing House*)

KARG-ELERT, S. (1877–1933): Op. 139a Jugend Musik for fl., cl., hn., pf. (*Zimmermann*); Op. 49, No. 1 Trio for ob., cl., cor ang. (*Hofmeister*); Wind quintet (*M.R.*)

KAUFFMANN, F. (1855–1934): Op. 40 Wind quintet (*Heinrichshofen*)

KAY, NORMAN FORBER: Miniature quartet for fl., cl., hn., bn. (*O.U.P.*)

KELEMEN, MILKO: Contrapuntal Etudes for wind quint. (*Schott*)

KELLER, H. (b. 1919): Five pieces for cl., bn. (*M.R.*)

KENNAWAY, LAMONT: Downstream for ob., cl., pf. (*Hinrichsen*)

KETTING, PIET (b. 1905): Trio for fl., cl., bn. (*Donemus*)

KING, HAROLD C.: Wind quintet (*Zimmermann*)

KITTL, J. B. (1806–68): Op. 25 Septet for wind quint., pf., db. (*Kistner*)

KLUGHARDT, A. F. M. (1847–1902): Op. 79 Wind quintet (*Zimmermann*)

KOECHLIN, C. (1867–1951): Idylle for 2 cl. (*Chant du Monde*); Trio for fl., cl., bn. (*Salabert*); Septet for fl., ob., cor ang., cl., alto sax., chromatic horn, bn. (*Oiseau Lyre*)

KOETSCHAU: Op. 12a Divertimento in B flat for fl., cl., bn. (*Hinrichsen*)

KOETSIER, JAN: 6 Bagatelles for ob., cl., bn. (*Donemus*)

KONSTANTINOFF: Trio for ob., cl., bn. (*De Wolfe*)

KOPPEL, H. (b. 1908): Sextet for wind quint., pf. (*Skandinavisk*)

KOPSCH, J. (b. 1887): Trio for ob., cl., pf. (*U.E.*)

KREJKI, I.: Divertimento for fl., cl., trpt., bn. (*M.R.*)

KŘENEK, ERNST (b. 1900): Sonatina for fl., cl. (*M.R.*)

KREUTZER, K.: Trio for cl., bn., pf. (*Hofmeister*)

KRIENS, C. (1881–1934): Ronde des Lutins for fl., ob., cl. (*Fischer*)

KROMMER, FR. (1759–1831): Partita for 2 cl., 2 hn., 2 bn. (*Hofmeister*)

KUBIK, GAIL (b. 1914): Little Suite for fl. & 2 cl. (*U.S.*)

KUBIZEK, A.: Wind quintet (*Döblinger*); Four Pieces for fl., cl., bn. (or ob., cl., bcl.) (*Br & H.*)

KUMMER, K. (b. 1795); Op. 46 2 Duos for fl., cl. (*André*); Trio for fl., cl., bn. (*Schott*)

KUNERT, K.: Two wind quintets (*Hofmeister*); Divertimento for wind quint. (*Hofmeister*); Sonata for cl., bn. (*Hofmeister*)

LACHNER, F. (1803–90): Op. 156 Octet for fl., ob., 2 cl., 2 hn., 2 bn. (*Kistner*)

LADMIRAULT, P. (1877–1944): Choral et Variations for wind quint., pf. (*Lemoine*)

LAHUSEN: Kleine Pfeifermusik zum Blasen Fiedeln und Tanzen für 2 cl. (*B. & H.*)

LAJTHA, L. (b. 1892): Quatre Hommages for fl., ob., cl., bn. (*U.M.P.*)

LANDRÉ, GUILLAUME: Wind quintet (*Donemus*)

LANGE, F. G. (nineteenth–twentieth century): Nonet for fl., 2 ob., 2 cl., 2 hn., 2 bn. (*Seeling*)

LANGE, H. (b. 1884): Serenade for ob., cl., hn., bn. (*M.R.*)

LAUBER, J. (1864–1952): Quatre Intermezzi for fl., cor ang., cl., bn. (*U.M.P.*)

LAURISCHKUS, M. (1876–1929): Op. 23 Suite for wind quint. (*Simrock*); Suite for fl., ob., cl., cor ang., 2 hn., 2 bn. (*Simrock*)

LAZZARI, S. (1857–1944): Octet for fl., ob., cl., cor ang., 2 hn., 2 bn. (*Evette & Schaeffer*)

LECHTHALER, JOSEF: Op. 53 Freundliche Abendmusik for fl., cl., guitar (or pf.) (*Anton Böhm*)

LEEUW, TON DE: Trio for fl., cl., pf. (*Donemus*)

LEFÈBVRE, C. E. (1843–1917): Op. 57 Suite for wind quint. (*Hamelle*)

LENDVAI, E. (1882–1949): Op. 23 Wind quintet (*Simrock*)

LEWIN, GORDON: Three Latin-American Impressions for fl., cl. (*B. & H.*); Nostalgia d'Espana for fl. & cl. (*B. & H.*); Scherzola for ob., cl., bn. (*New Wind Music*)

LILIEN, IGNACE (b. 1897): Apollinisch Sonatine for 2 fl., 2 ob., 2 cl., 2 bn., 2 hn. (*Donemus*)

LINDNER: Wind quintet (*Hofmeister*)

LIPATTI, DINU (1917–50): Aubade for fl., ob., cl., bn. (*Schott*)

LLOYD, CHARLES (1849–1919): Suite for cl., bn., pf. (*Rudall Carte*)

LORENZO, LEONARDO DE: Op. 76 Trio Eccentrico for fl., cl., bn. (*Hinrichsen*)

LUENING, OTTO: Fuguing Tune for wind quint. (*U.S.*)

LUTYENS, ELISABETH (b. 1906): Wind quintet (*Mills*)

MAASZ, GERHARD: Divertimento for fl., cl., bn. (*Sikorski*)

MACDONALD, MALCOLM (cont. British): Divertimento for wind quint. (*MS.*)

MAESSEN, ANTOON: Cassation for ob., cl., bn. (*Donemus*); Trio for fl., cl., bn. (*Donemus*)

MAGNARD, A. (1865–1914): Op. 8 Quintet for fl., ob., cl., bn., pf. (*Salabert*)

MALIPIERO, G. F. (b. 1882): Sonata for fl., ob., cl., bn. (*Universal*)

MALIPIERO, R. (b. 1914): Chamber Music for wind quint. (*Suvini Zerboni*)

MAROS, RUDOLF: Serenata for ob., cl., bn. (*Budapest*)

MARTELLI, H. (b. 1895): Trio for ob., cl., bn (*Costallat*)

MARTINON, J. (b. 1910): Sonatine No. 4 for ob., cl., bn. (*Costallat*)

MARTINU, B. (1890–1959): 4 Madrigale for ob., cl., bn. (*Schott*); Wind quintet (*Chester*)

MASSÉUS, JAN: Introduction and Allegro for ob., cl., pf. (*Donemus*)

MATZATZEN: Uzbek Folk-Song for fl., cl., and pf. (*U.S.S.R. State Music*)

MAW, NICHOLAS (b. 1935): Chamber Music for ob., cl., bn., hn., pf. (*Chester*)

MEDERACKE, K.: Bohemian Suite for wind quint. (*Hofmeister*)

MELCHIOR, A. J. B. (nineteenth century): Op. 1 and 8 Two quartets for fl., cl., hn., bn. (*Lemoine*)

MENDELSSOHN, F. (1809–47): Op. 113 Zwei Konzertstücke for cl., basset-horn, pf. (*Br. & H.*)

MENGAL, M. J. (b. 1784): Op. 18 and 19 Works include 6 Quartets for fl., cl., hn., bn. (*Lemoine*)

MENGELBERG, K. (1892–1959): Trio for ob., cl., bn. (*Donemus*)

MICHAEL, EDWARD: Sonatine for fl., cl. (*Ricordi*)

MIGOT, GEORGES (b. 1891): Trio for ob., cl., bn. (*Leduc*); Threne for ob., cl., bn. (*U.M.P.*); Wind quintet (*U.M.P.*)

MIHAILOVICI, M. (b. 1898): Op. 35 Sonate for E flat cl., A cl., bcl. (*U.M.P.*)

MILHAUD, D. (b. 1892): Pastorale for ob., cl., bn. (*Chant du Monde*); Suite d'après Corrette for ob., cl., bn. (*Oiseau Lyre*); Sonata for fl., ob., cl., pf. (*Durand*); La Cheminée du Roi René for wind quint. (*Andraud*)

MIRANDOLLE, L. (cont. French): Quartet for fl., ob., cl., bn. (*Leduc*); Quartet for 2 cl., alto cl., bcl. (*MS.*)

MIROUZE, M. (cont. French): Pièce en septuor for fl., ob., cl., hn., bn., trpt., pf. (*Leduc*)

MORITZ, E. (b. 1891): Wind quintet (*Zimmermann*); Divertimento for fl., cl., bn. (*Zimmermann*)

MORTENSEN, O.: Wind quintet (*Hansen*)

MOZART (1756–91): K.A. 229 5 Divertimenti for 2 cl., bn. (*Br. & H.*); K. 487 12 Duets for 2 basset-horns (*Br. & H.*); K. 452 Quintet for ob., cl., hn., bn., pf. (*Hinrichsen*); K. 411 Adagio for 2 cl., 3 basset-horns (*Br. & H.*); K. 375 and 388 Serenades for 2 ob., 2 cl., 2 hn., 2 bn. (*Br. & H.*); K. 361 Serenade for 2 ob., 2 cl., 2 basset-horns, 2 bn., 4 hn., contra-bn. (or db.) (*Br. & H*); K. 166 & 186, Divertimenti Nos. 3 & 4 for 2 ob., 2 cor ang., 2 cl., 2 bn., 2 hn. (*Br. & H.*)

MULDER, ERNEST W. (b. 1898): Sextet for wind quint., pf. (*Donemus*); Fugue VII from 'Ars Contrapunctica' for fl., cl., bn. (*Donemus*)

MÜLLER, P. (b. 1898): Three wind quintets (*Ruhle*)

MUNGEN, O.: Trio for fl., cl., pf. (*M.R.*)

NIELSEN, CARL (1865–1931): Op. 43 Wind quintet (*Hansen*)

NILSSON, BO. (b. 1937): 20 'Gruppen' for picc., fl., ob., cl. (*U.E.*)

NOCENTINI, D.: 14 Duetti for 2 cl. (*Carisch*)

NONO, LUIGI (b. 1924): Polifonia—Monodia—Ritmica for fl., cl., bcl., sax., hn., pf., perc. (*Schott*)

NOVAČEK, R. (1866–1900): Op. 48 Sinfonietta for fl., ob., 2 cl., 2 hn., 2 bn. (*Br. & H.*)

OLSEN, SPARRE (cont. Norwegian): Op. 35 Wind quintet (*Harald Lyche*); Op. 10 Suite for fl., ob., cl. (*Harald Lyche*)

ONSLOW, G. (1784–1853): Op. 81 Wind quintet (*Br. & H.*); Op. 30 Sextet for fl., cl., hn., bn., pf., db. (*Br. & H.*)

ORBAN, MARCEL: Prelude, Pastorale & Divertissement for ob., cl., bn.

OSIECK, HANS: Divertimento for wind quint. & pf. (*Donemus*)

PARRY, HUBERT (1898–1918): Nonet for fl., 2 ob., 2 cl., 2 bn., 2 hn. (*MS.*)

PASCAL (cont. French): Octet for 2 fl., ob., cl., 2 bn., hn., trpt. (*Durand*)

PAUER, J. (b. 1891): Divertimento for 3 cl. (*M.R.*)

PEETERS, FLOR (b. 1903): Op. 80 Trio for fl., cl., bn. (*Hinrichsen*)

PERCEVAL, J.: Serenade for fl., cl., bn. (*M.R.*)

PÉRILHOU, A.: Divertissement for 2 fl., 2 cl. (*Heugel*)

PERSICHETTI, VINCENT: Pastoral for wind quint. (*Schirmer*)

PESSARD, E. (1843–1917): Op. 6 Aubade for wind quint. (*Leduc*)

PFEIFFER, G. J. (1835–1908): Musette for ob., cl., bn. (*Rouart, Lerolle*)

PHILLIPS, GORDON (cont. British): Suite for ob., cl. (*Schott*); Pastoral for fl., ob., cl. (*Hinrichsen*)

PIERNÉ, G. (1863–1937): Pastorale for wind quint. (*Leduc*); Suite Pittoresque for wind quint. (*Leduc*); Op. 30 Pastorale Variée for fl., ob., cl., hn., 2 bn., trpt. (*Durand*); Op. 40, No. 1 Preludio e Fughetta for 2 fl., ob., cl., hn., 2 bn. (*Hamelle*)

PIERNÉ, P. (cont. French): Bucolique Variée for ob., cl., bn. (*Costallat*); Suite Pittoresque for wind quint. (*U.M.P.*)

PIJPER, W. (1894–1947): Trio for fl., cl., bn. (*Donemus*); Wind quintet (*Donemus*); Sextet for fl., ob., cl., hn., bn., pf. (*Donemus*); Septet for wind quint., pf., db. (*Donemus*)

PIKET, F. (cont. American): Legend and Jollity for 3 cl. (*Omega*); Reflection and Caprice for 4 cl. (*Omega*)

PISTON, WALTER (b. 1894): Three Pieces for fl., cl., bn. (*Albert Andraud, Ohio*)

POHL, JOSEF: Rosa und Röschen for fl., cl., pf. (*Seeling*)

POLDOWSKI (1880–1932): Octet for 2 fl., ob., ob. d'amore, cor ang., cl., basset-horn, bcl. (*MS.*)

PONSE, LUCTOR: Two Pieces for wind quint. (*Donemus*); Trio for fl., cl., bn. (*Donemus*)

POOT, MARCEL (b. 1901): Ballade for ob., cl., bn. (*Schott*); Divertimento for ob., cl., bn. (*Schott*)

POSTON, ELIZABETH (b. 1905): Trio for fl., cl., hp. (or pf.) (*Chester*)

POULENC, F. (1899–1963): Sonata for 2 cl. (*Chester*); Sonata for cl., bn. (*Chester*); Sextet for wind quint., pf. (*Hansen*); Trio for ob., cl., bn. (*Hansen*)

PRAAG, H. VAN: 2 wind quintets (*Donemus*); Quartet for fl., ob., cl., bn. (*Donemus*); Drie schetsen for fl., ob., cl., bn. (*Donemus*); Three Sketches for 2 ob., 2 cl., 2 bn., 2 hn. (*Donemus*)

PROKOFIEV, S. (1891–1953): Fleeting Moments for fl., ob., cl., bn. (*M.R.*)

RAFF, J. (1822–82): Op. 188 Sinfonietta for 2 fl., 2 ob., 2 cl., 2 hn., 2 bn. (*Siegel*)

RAINIER, PRIAULX (b. 1903): Six Pieces for wind quint. (*Schott*)

RANDERSON (nineteenth–twentieth century): Wind quintet (*Durand*)

RAWSTHORNE, ALAN (b. 1905): Quintet for ob., cl., bn., hn., pf. (*O.U.P.*)

READ, GARDNER (b. 1913): Scherzino for wind quint. (*U.S.*)

REGNER, HERMANN: Divertimento for E flat cl., fl. (*Hinrichsen*)

REICHA, A. (1770–1836): Quintets for wind (*Simrock*)

REINECKE, C. (1824–1910): Op. 274 Trio for cl., hn., pf. (*Senff*); Op. 271 Sextet for fl., ob., cl., 2 hn., bn. (*Zimmermann*); Op. 216 Octet for fl., ob., 2 cl., 2 hn., 2 bn. (*Kistner*)

REIZENSTEIN, FRANZ (b. 1911): Wind quintet (*B. & H.*); Serenade in F for fl., 2 ob., 2 cl., 2 hn., 2 bn., db. (*B. & H.*)

RENZI, ARMANDO: 5 Bagatelles for wind quint. (*de Santis*)

REUTER, F.: Spielmusik for cl., bn., 1936 (*Kistner*)

RHENÉ-BATON (1879–1940): Op. 53 Aubade for fl., ob., 2 cl., hn., 2 bn. (*Durand*)

RIEGGER, W. (b. 1885): Wind quintet (*Schott*)

RIETHMULLER, R.: Miniatures for fl., cl., bn. (*M.R.*)

RIJSAGER, K.: (b. 1897): Quartet for fl., ob., cl., bn. (*M.R.*)

RIMSKY-KORSAKOV, N. (1844–1908): Quintet for fl., cl., hn., bn., pf. (*Belaieff*); Canzonetta & Tarantella for 2 cl. (*M.R.*)

RIVIER, J. (b. 1896): Petite Suite for ob., cl., bn. (*Fougères*)

ROE, CHRISTOPHER: Three Bagatelles for 2 cl. (*New Wind Music*)

RÖNTGEN, JULIUS (1855–1932): Serenade for wind quint.; Op. 14 Serenade for fl., ob., cl., 2 hn., 2 bn. (*U.E.*); Op. 86 Trio for fl., ob., bn. (*Alsbach*)

DE ROOS, ROBERT (b. 1907): Sextuor for wind quint., pf. (*Donemus*)

ROPARTZ, G. (b. 1864): Deux Pièces for wind quint. (*Durand*); Entrata e Scherzetto for ob., cl., bn. (*Salabert*)

RORICH, K. (b. 1869): Op. 81*b* Suite for fl., cl., bn. (*Zimmermann*); Op. 58 Wind quintet (*Zimmermann*)

ROSETTI, F. A. (1746–92): Partita for 2 ob., 2 cl., bn., 2 hn. (*Kneussling, Zurich*); Wind quint. in E flat (*Hinrichsen*)

ROSSINI, G. (1792–1868): 6 Quartets for fl., cl., hn., bn. (*Schott*)

ROTA: Petite Offrande Musicale for wind quint. (*U.M.P.*)

ROUGNON: Andante and Polonaise for ob., cl., pf. (*Leduc*)

ROUSSEL, A. (1869–1937): Op. 6 Divertissement for wind quint., pf. (*Salabert*)

ROWLEY, ALEC (1892–1958): Nocturne for 4 cl. (*Augener*)

RUEFF: Three Pieces for ob., cl., bn. (*U.M.P.*)

SAINT-SAËNS, C. (1835–1921): Caprice on Danish Airs for fl., ob., cl., pf. (*Leduc*); Feuillet d'Album for fl., ob., 2 cl., 2 hn., 2 bn. (*Leduc*)

SALOME, T. C. (1834–96): Canon Marziale for fl., ob., cl., bn. (*Mills*)

SANGIORGI, ALFREDO (cont. Italian): Duo-Sonata for cl., bn. (*Forlivesi, Florence*)

SAUGUET, H. (b. 1901): Trio for ob., cl., bn. (*Oiseau Lyre*)

SCHIERBECK: Op. 53 Capriccio for wind quint.

SCHISKE, K. (b. 1916): Op. 24 Wind quint. (*U.E.*)

SCHMID, H. K. (cont. German): Op. 28 Wind quintet, 1921 (*Schott*)

SCHMIDT, F. (1874–1939): Serenade for fl., ob., cl. (*Hieber*)

SCHMITT, F. (1870–1958): Sonatine en Trio for fl., cl., pf. (*Durand*); Lied and Scherzo for double wind quint. (including solo horn) (*Durand*); A Tours d'Anches for ob., cl., bn., pf. (*Durand*); Sextet for 6 cl.: E flat, 2 B flat, alto, bass, contra bass (*Durand*)

SCHNEIDER: Old Dutch Dance-Suite for 3 cl. (*U.E.*); Partita for 2 cl. (*U.E.*)

SCHÖNBERG, A. (1874–1951): Op. 26 Wind quintet (*U.E.*)

SCHOUWMAN, HANS (b. 1902): Op. 36 Trio for cl., bn., pf. (*Donemus*)

SCHRECK, GUSTAV: Op. 40 Nonet for 2 fl., ob., 2 cl., 2 hn., 2 bn. (*Br. & H.*)

SCHROEDER, H.: Op. 36 Sextet for wind quint. & pf. (*Schott*)

SCHUBERT, F. (1797–1828): D. 72 Minuet & Finale for 2 ob., 2 cl., 2 hn., 2 bn. (*Br. & H.*)

SCHULHOFF, E. (1894–1942): Divertissement for ob., cl., bn. (*Schott*)

SCHULLER, GUNTHER (b. 1927): Suite for wind quint. (*Hinrichsen*)

SCHULTZ, SVEND (b. 1913): Une Amourette (Petite Serenade) for wind quint. (*Skandinavisk*)

SEHLBACH, E.: Serenade for wind quint. (*Moseler Verlag*)

SEIBER, MÁTYÁS (1905–60): Permutazione a Cinque for wind quint. (*Schott*); Serenade for 2 cl., 2 bn., 2 hn. (*Hansen*)

SHEINKMAN: Divertimento for cl., trpt., tromb., hp. (*Hinrichsen*)

SIBINGA, TH. H. SMIT: Plain Music for fl., ob., cl. (*Donemus*)

SLAVICKY, K. (b. 1910): Trio for ob., cl., bn. (*Hudebni*)

SMIT, LEO (b. 1921): Sextuor for wind quint., pf. (*Donemus*)

SOBECK, J. (nineteenth–twentieth century): Op. 11 and 14 Two Wind quintets (*Bosworth*); Duo for cl., hn., pf. (*Böte & Bock*)

SODDERLAND, JAN: Sonatine for fl., cl. (*Donemus*)

SOURIS: Rengaines for wind quint. (*U.M.P.*)

SOWERBY, L. (b. 1895): Wind quintet (*Schirmer*)

SOWFFRIAN, A.: Op. 30 Sonata for 2 cl. (*Brogneaux*)

SPOHR, L. (1784–1859): Op. 52 Quintet for fl., cl., hn., bn., pf. (*Br. & H.*)

STADEN, J. (1581–1634) (arr. Bonsel): Venus-Kraentzlein, Suite for cor ang., fl., ob., cl., hn. (*De Wolfe*)

STAINER, C. (early twentieth century): Scherzo for wind quint. (*B. & H.*)

STAMITZ, K. (1717–57): Quartet for ob., cl., hn., bn. (*Br. & H.*)

STARK, R. (nineteenth century): Op. 55 Serenade for 2 cl., 2 bn. (*Hinrichsen*); Original Sonata in G minor for 2 cl., basset-horn (*Hinrichsen*)

STIEBER, H.: Spielmusik No. 2 for 2 fl., cl. (*Hofmeister*); Octet for fl., 2 ob., 2 cl., hn., 2 bn. (*Hofmeister*)

STOCKHAUSEN, K. (b. 1928): Zeitmasse for fl., ob., cor ang., cl., bn. (*U.E.*)

STRATEGIER, HERMANN (b. 1912): Sextet for wind quint., pf. (*Donemus*)

STRAVINSKY, I. (b. 1882): Octet for fl., cl., 2 bn., 2 trpt., 2 tromb. (*B. & H.*)

SUSATO (sixteenth century) (arr. Bonsel): Old Dutch Dances for wind quint. (*De Wolfe*)

SUTERMEISTER, H. (b. 1910): Serenade for 2 cl., trpt., bn. (*Schott*)

SZALOWSKI, A. (b. 1923): Duo for fl., cl. (*Omega*); Trio for ob., cl., bn. (*Omega*); Divertimento for ob., cl., bn. (*Chester*)

SZÉKÉLY, ENDRE: Wind quintet (*Mills*)

SZELIGOWSKI, T.: Wind quintet (*Polish State Publishing House*)

TAFFANEL, C. P. (1844–1908): Wind quintet (*Leduc*)

TAK, P. C.: Prelude, Chorale & Fugue for fl., cl., bn. (*Donemus*)

TANSMAN, A. (b. 1897): Dans de la Sorcière for wind quint., pf. (*Eschig*); Hexentanz from *Le Jardin du Paradis* for wind quint., pf. (*Schott*); Four Impressions for 2 fl., 2 ob., 2 cl., 2 bn. (*M.R.*); Suite for ob., cl., bn. (*Schott*)

THUILLE, L. (1861–1907): Op. 6 Sextet for wind quint., pf. (*Br.&H.*)

TOJA, G. (seventeenth century): Serenade for fl., ob., 2 cl., 2 hn., bn. (*Ricordi*)

TOMASI, H. (b. 1901): Concert Champêtre for ob., cl., bn. (*Leduc*); Wind quintet (*Leduc*); Variations sur un Thème Corse for wind quint. (*Leduc*)

TOMLINSON, ERNEST (b. 1924): Divertimento for fl., ob., cl., bcl., bn. (*MS.*); Concertino for double wind quint. (*MS.*)

TOVEY, D. F. (1875–1940): Op. 8 Trio for cl., hn., pf. (*Schott*)

TOWNSEND, DOUGLAS: Ballet Suite for 3 cl. (*Hinrichsen*)

TROJAN, VÁCLAV: Wind quintet (*Czech State Publishing House*)

TSCHEREPNIN, A. (b. 1899): Trio for 3 cl. (*M.R.*)

TURECHEK: Introduction and Scherzo for wind quint. (*Witmark*)

TUSTIN, W. (cont. American): Tarantella and Scherzo for fl., ob., cl. (*Barnhouse, U.S.A.*)

UHL, ALFRED (b. 1909): Octet (*Eine Vergnügliche Musik*) for 2 ob., 2 cl., 2 hn., 2 bn. (*U.E.*); Divertimento for 3 cl., bcl. (*Schott*)

VALEN, FARTEIN (1887–1952): Op. 42 Serenade for wind quint. (*Hinrichsen*)

VALENTINI, G. (twentieth century): Quartettino for fl., ob., cl., bn. (*Mignani*)

VARÈSE, E. (b. 1885): Octandre for fl., ob., cl., bn., hn., trpt., tromb., db. (*Ricordi*)

VASILENKO, S. (b. 1872): Op. 65 Quartet (on Turkish Folk-tunes) for fl., ob., cl., bn. (*U.E.*)

VELDEN, R. VAN DER: Second Concerto for wind quint. (*Hinrichsen*)

VERESS, SANDOR (b. 1907): Sonatina for ob., cl., bn. (*Suvini Zerboni*)

VERHAAR, ARY: Op. 38 Trio for fl., ob., cl. (*Donemus*)

VILLA-LOBOS, H. (1887–1959): Choros No. 2 for fl., cl. (*Eschig*); Trio for ob., cl., bn. (*Schott*); Choros No. 7 for fl., ob., cl., sax., bn. (*Eschig*); Fantasie Concertante for cl., bn., pf. (*Schott*); Quintet en forme de Choros for wind quint. (*Schott*); Quartet for fl., ob., cl., bn. (*Schott*)

VINTER, GILBERT (cont. British): Two Miniatures for wind quint. (*B. & H.*)

VOGEL, WLADIMIR (b. 1896): Ticinella: Folk Tunes from Tessin (Switzerland) for fl., ob., cl., sax., bn. (*Suvini Zerboni*)

VOXMANN, H. (b. 1912): Chamber music for 3 cl. (*M.R.*)

WAILLY, P. DE (1854–1933): Aubade for fl., ob., cl. (*Salabert*); Octet for fl., ob., 2 cl., 2 bn., hn., trpt. (*Rouart*)

WALCKIERS, E. (b. 1793): Op. 7 Three Quartets for fl., cl., hn., bn. (*Costallat*); Op. 48 Quartet for fl., cl., hn., bn. (*Schlesinger*); Op. 12 3 Trios for fl., cl., bn. (*Costallat*)

WALTHEW, R. H. (1872–1951): Triolet for ob., cl., bn. (*B. & H.*)

WARD, WILLIAM: Little Dance Suite for wind quint. (*Mills*)

WATERSON, J.: Grand quartet for 4 cl. (*Mahillon*)

WEBER, ALAIN: Trio for ob., cl., bn. (*U.M.P.*); Wind quintet (*U.M.P.*)

WEEGENHUISE, JOHAN: Tre pezzi for fl., cl. (*Donemus*)

WEIS, FLEMING (b. 1898): Serenade for wind quint. (*Hansen*)

WEISS, A. (b. 1891): Trio for fl., cl., bn. (*Chester*)

WELLESZ, EGON (b. 1885): Op. 73 Suite for wind quint. (*U.E.*)

WERTHEIM, ROSY: Trio for fl., ob., cl. (*Donemus*)

WHETTAM, GRAHAM (cont. British): Op. 19 Wind quintet (*De Wolfe*); Divertimento No. 1 for ob., cl., bn. (*De Wolfe*); Fantasy Sextet for wind quint., pf. (*De Wolfe*); Sinfonietta for 2 fl., 2 ob., 2 cl., 2 hn., 2 bn. (*De Wolfe*); Fantasy for Ten Instruments for double wind quint. (*MS.*)

WIENER, K.: Op. 20, No. 3 Piece for fl., cor ang., cl. (*U.E.*)

WIJDEVELD, WOLFGANG: Wind quintet (*Donemus*)

WILDGANS, F. (b. 1913): Little Trio for fl., cl., bn. (*U.E.*); Three Inventions for cl., hn. (*Döblinger*); Kleines Trio for fl., cl., bn. (*Döblinger*)

WILDSCHUT, CLARA: Kleine Serenade for wind quint. (*Donemus*)

WINNUBST, JOHAN: Kleine Serenade for wind quint. & pf. (*Donemus*)

WISSMER, P. (b. 1915): Trio for ob., cl., bn. (*Costallat*)

WOOD, CHARLES (1866–1926): Wind quintet in F (*B. & H.*)

ZAGWIJN, HENRI (b. 1878): Trio for ob., cl., pf. (*Donemus*); 2 Trios for fl., ob., cl. (*Donemus*); Suite for wind quint., pf. (*Donemus*); Scherzo for wind quint., pf. (*Donemus*)

ZBINDEN: Trio for ob., cl., bn. (*U.M.P.*)

ZENDER: Op. 3 Wind quintet (*Böte & Bock*)

ZILCHER, H. (1881–1948): Wind quintet (*Zimmermann*)

CLARINET AND STRINGS
(with or without other wind and piano)

ACHRON, J. (1886–1943): Op. 57 Children's Suite for cl., str. qt., pf. (*U.E.*)

AMBERG, J., (b. 1846): Op. 12 Fantasiestücke for cl., va., pf. (*Hansen*); Op. 11 Trio for cl., vc., pf. (*Hansen*)

ANDRIESSEN, JURIAAN (b. 1925): Hommage à Milhaud for fl., ob., cl., bn., hn., trpt., tromb., sax., vn., va., vc. (*Donemus*)

ARDEVAL, J.: Two Sonatas for ob., cl., vc. (*M.R.*)

BAAREN, KEES VAN: Sextet for wind quint., vc., db. (*Donemus*)

BACH, W. F. E. (1759–1845): Sextet in E flat for cl., 2 hn., vn., va., vc. (*Hinrichsen*)

BADINGS, HENK (b. 1907): Octet for cl., bn., hn., 2 vn., va., vc., db. (*Donemus*)

BAERMANN, H. (1784–1847): Op. 18 Quintet for cl., str. qt. (*Schott*)

BANKS, DON (b. 1923): Sonata da Camera for 8 instruments for fl., cl., bcl., vn., va., vc., pf., perc. (*Schott*)

BARTÓK, BÉLA (1881–1945): Constrasts for cl., vn., pf. (*B. & H.*)

BAX, ARNOLD (1883–1953): Nonet for fl., ob., cl., hp., str. qt., db. (*Chappell*)

BEETHOVEN, L. VAN (1770–1827): Op. 11 Trio for cl., vc., pf.; Op. 38 Trio (arr. by the composer from the Septet Op. 20) for cl., vc., pf.; Op. 20 Septet for cl., hn., bn., vn., va., vc., db.

BENTZON, J. (1897–1948): Op. 24 Intermezzo for cl., vn. (*Hansen*); Op. 12 Variazioni Interrotti for cl., bn., vn., va., vc. (*Hansen*)

BEREZOVSKY, N. (b. 1900): Op. 7 Theme and Variations for cl., str. qt., pf. (*Ed. Russe*)

BERG, ALBAN (1885–1935): Adagio for vn., cl., pf., from the Chamber Concerto (*U.E.*)

BERGER, W. (1861–1911): Op. 94 Trio for cl., vc., pf. (*Kahnt*)

BERIO, LUCIANO (b. 1925): Differences for fl., cl., va., vc., hp. & stereophonic tape (*Suvini Zerboni*)

BERKELEY, LENNOX (b. 1903): Sextet for cl., hn., str. qt. (*Chester*)

BLATT, F. (1793–?): Theme and Variations for cl., str. qt. (*Simrock*)

BLISS, ARTHUR (b. 1891): Quintet for cl., str. qt. (*Novello*)

BLOMDAHL, KARL-BIRGER (b. 1916): Trio for cl., vc., pf. (*Schott*)

BOCHSA, C. (d. 1821): Trois Quatuors concertans for cl., vn., va., vc. (*Monsigny*)

BORRIS, S.: Kleine Suite for fl., ob. (cor ang.), cl., bn., vn., va., vc. (*Sirius*)

BOWEN, YORK (1884–1961): Fantasy-Quintet for bcl., str. qt. (*De Wolfe*); Septet for cl., hn., pf., str. qt.

BRAHMS, J. (1833–97): Op. 114 Trio for cl., vc., pf.; Op. 115 Quintet for cl., str. qt.

BREUER, K.: Antonalyse for cl., str. (*M.R.*)

BROWN, EARLE: Pentathis for 9 Solo Instruments for fl., bcl., trpt., tromb., hp., pf., vn., va., vc. (*Schott*)

BRUCH, MAX (1838–1920): Op. 83 Acht Stücke for cl., va., pf. (*Simrock*)

BRUSTAD, BJARNE (b. 1895): Trio No. 2 for vn., cl., bn.

BUSCH, A. (1891–1952): Op. 26 Nos. 1 & 2 Hausmusik for cl., vn. (*Br. & H.*); Op. 26, No. 3 Deutsche Tänze for cl., va., vc. (*Br. & H.*)

BUSH, GEOFFREY (b. 1920): Rhapsody for cl., str. qt. (*Elkin*)

BUTTERWORTH, ARTHUR (cont. British): Modal Suite for fl., cl., bn., trpt., vn. (*Hinrichsen*)

CASELLA, ALFREDO (1883–1947): Serenata for cl., trpt., bn., vn., vc. (*U.E.*); Op. 54 Sinfonia for cl., trpt., vc., pf.

CASTÉRA, R. DE (b. 1873): Concerto for fl., cl., vc., pf. (*Salabert*)

CHEMIN-PETIT: Short Suite for 9 instruments for ob., cl., bn., 2 vn., va., vc., db., timp. (*Hinrichsen*)

COLERIDGE-TAYLOR, S. (1875–1912): Op. 15 Quintet for cl., str. qt. (*Br. & H.*)

COOKE, ARNOLD (b. 1906): Quintet for cl., str. qt. (*O.U.P.*); Quintet for fl., cl., vn., vc., hp. (*MS.*)

COPLAND, AARON (b. 1900): Sextet for cl., str. qt., pf. (*B. & H.*)

CRUSELL, B. (1775–1838): Op. 2, 4, & 7 Quatuors for cl., vn., va., vc. (*Peters*)

DAHL, INGOLF: Concerto a Tre for cl., vn., vc. (*U.S.*)

DANEAU, SUZANNE: Contrasts for fl., ob., cl., bn., va., vc., hp. (*De Wolfe*)

DAVID, J. N. (b. 1895): Op. 23 No. 4 Sonata for cl., va. (*M.R.*)

DAVIES, PETER MAXWELL (b. 1934): Sextet for fl., cl., bcl., vn., vc., pf. (*Schott*); Ricercar and Doubles on 'To many a Well' for wind quint. va., vc. & harpsichord (*Schott*)

DESSAU, PAUL: Concertino for fl., cl., hn., vn. (*Schott*)

DIAMOND, D. (b. 1915): Quintet for cl., 2 va., 2 vc. (*M.R.*)

DIJK, JAN VAN: Trio for cl., va., vc. (*Donemus*)

DOBRYNSKI, I. F.: Duet for cl., vc. (*Polish State Publishing House*)

DOHNANYI, E. (b. 1877): Op. 37 Sextet for pf., vn., va., vc., cl., hn. (*Lengnick*)

DOUGLAS, ROY (b. 1907): Trio Movement for cl., va., pf. (*Hinrichsen*)

DUBOIS, T. (1837-1924): Nonet for fl., ob., cl., bn., str. qt., db. (*Heugel*)

DUNHILL, T. F. (1877-1946): Op. 3 Quintet for cl., hn., vn., vc., pf. (*B. & H.*)

DVOŘÁK, A. (1841-1904): Op. 44 Serenade for 2 ob., 2 cl., 3 hn., 2 bn., vc., db. (*Simrock*)

DYSON, GEORGE (b. 1883): Quartet for cl., hn., vn., pf. (*MS.*)

EBERL, A. (1766-1807): Op. 36 Trio for cl., vc., pf. (*Kühnel*)

EDER, HELMUT: Op. 25 Quintet for cl., str. qt. (*M.R.*); Quartet for cl., vn., va., vc. (*M.R.*); Op. 33 Ottetto breve for fl., ob., cl., bn., str. qt. (*Döblinger*)

ENGEL, J.: Suite 1 for cl., str. quintet (*M.R.*)

ETLER, ALVIN: Quartet for ob., cl., bn., va. (*U.S.*); Sonata for ob., cl., va. (*U.S.*); Quartet for ob., cl., va., bn. (*M.R.*)

FALLA, M. DE (1876-1946): Concerto for harpsichord, fl., ob., cl., vn., vc. (*Eschig*)

FARRENC, L. (1804-75): Op. 44 Trio for cl., vc., pf. (*Leduc*)

FERGUSON, HOWARD (b. 1908): Octet for cl., bn., hn., 2 vn., va., vc., db. (*B. & H.*)

FIBICH, Z. (1850-1900): Op. 42 Quintet for cl., hn., vn., vc. (*Urbánek*)

FLOTHUIS, MARIUS (b. 1914): Divertimento for cl., bn., hn., vn., va., db. (*Donemus*)

FRANKEL, BENJAMIN (b. 1905): Trio for cl., vc., pf. (*Augener*); Op. 28 Quintet for cl., str. qt. (*Chester*)

FRICKER, PETER RACINE (b. 1910): Op. 30 Octet for fl., cl., bn., hn., vn., va., vc., db. (*Schott*)

FROMM, MICHAELS I.: Musica Larga for cl., str. qt. (*M.R.*)

FRÜHLING, C.: Trio for cl., vc., pf. (*M.R.*)

FUCHS, R. (1847–1927): Op. 102 Quintet for cl., str. qt. (*Robitschek*)

GAL, HANS (b. 1890): Serenade for cl., vn., vc. (*MS.*)

GENZMER, HARALD (b. 1909): Septet for fl., cl., hn., vn., va., vc., hp. (*Schott*)

GHEDINI, G. F. (b. 1892): Adagio e Allegro da Concerto for fl., cl., hn., vn., va., vc., hp. (*Ricordi*)

GILSE, JAN VAN (1881–1944): Nonet for ob., cl., bn., hn., str. qt., db. (*Donemus*)

GIPPS, RUTH (b. 1921): Rhapsody in E flat for cl., str. qt. (*MS.*)

GLIERE, REINHOLD (b. 1875) (arr. John Bath): Morning, for fl., ob., cl., hp., str. qt. (*De Wolfe*)

GODRON, HUGO (cont. Dutch): Sérénade Occidentale for cl., vn., pf. (*Donemus*)

GOEHR, ALEXANDER (b. 1932): Op. 11 Suite for Chamber ensemble for vn., vc., fl., cl., hn., hp. (*Schott*)

GOLDBERG, THEO: Op. 7 Quintet for cl., str. qt. (*Böte & Bock*)

GUNDRY, INGLIS (b. 1905): Duo for cl., vc. (*Hinrichsen*)

HAAN, STEFAN DE (cont. British): Suite for ob., vn., cl., vc. (*Hinrichsen*)

HAMILTON, IAIN (b. 1922): Op. 2 Quintet for cl., str. qt. (*Schott*)

HARRISON, PAMELA (b. 1915): Quintet for cl., str. qt. (*MS.*)

HARSÁNYI, T. (b. 1898): Nonet for fl., ob., cl., bn., hn., str. qt. (*La Sirène*)

HARTMAN, EMIL (1836–98): Op. 24 Serenade for cl., vc., pf. (*Simon*)

HAUER, J. M. (b. 1883): Op. 26 Quintet for cl., vn., va., vc., pf. (*Lienau*)

HAWTHORNE-BAKER, A: Threnody for ob., cl., hn., hp., vn., va., vc. (*Hinrichsen*)

HEILLER, A. (b. 1923): Sextet for ob., cl., bn., vn., va., vc. (*U.E.*)

HEMEL, OSCAR VAN: Quintet for cl., str. qt. (*Donemus*)

HEPPENER, ROBERT: Septet for fl., cl., bn., 2 vn., va., vc. (*Donemus*)

HÉROLD: Serenade for cl., va., vc. (*Schmidt*)

HERRMANN, E.: Serenata for ob., cl., str. qt. (*Raabe*)

HINDEMITH, PAUL (b. 1895): Zwei Stücke for cl., vn. (*Schott*); Quartet for cl., vn., vc., pf. (*Schott*); Variations for cl., vn., va., vc. (*Schott*); Drei Stücke for cl., trpt., vn., db., pf. (*Schott*); Op. 30 Quintet for cl., str. qt. (*Schott*); Octet for cl., bn., hn., vn., 2 va., vc., db. (*Schott*)

HODDINOTT, ALUN (b. 1929): Quartet for cl., vn., va., vc. (*MS.*)

HOLBROOKE, J. (b. 1878): Op. 27, No. 1 Quintet for cl., str. qt. (*Modern Music Library*); Op. 27, No. 2 Quintet for cl., str. qt. (*Modern Music Library*); Op. 57, No. 1 Nocturne, *Fairyland*, for cl., va., pf. (*Chester*)

HOLLER, KARL (b. 1907): Op. 46 Quintet for cl., str. qt. (*Müller*)

HOMS, JOACHIM: Trio for fl., vn., bcl.

HONEGGER, A. (1892–1955): 3 Contre points for cl., vn., vc. (*Chester*)

HOROVITZ, JOSEPH (b. 1926): Concertante for cl. & strings (*Chester*)

HOWELLS, HERBERT (b. 1892): Op. 31 Rhapsodic Quintet for cl., str. qt. (*S. & B.*)

HUMMEL, J. H.: Quartet in E flat for cl., vn., va., vc. (*MS.*)

HUMMEL, J. N. (1778–1837): Op. 114 Septet Militaire for fl., cl., trpt., vn., va., vc., pf. (*Haslinger*)

IBERT, J. (b. 1880): Two Interludes for cl., vn., pf. (or hp.) (*Chester*); Capriccio for wind quint., str. qt. (*Leduc*)

D'INDY, V. (1851–1931): Op. 29 Trio for cl., vc., pf. (*Hamelle*)

INGENHOVEN, J. (b. 1876): Trio for fl., cl., hp. (*Salabert*); Sonatina for cl., vn. (*Tischer & Jagenberg*)

IRELAND, JOHN (1879–1962): Sextet for cl., hn., str. qt. (*Augener*)

IVES, CHARLES (1874–1954): Largo (1901) for vn., cl., pf. (*Southern Music Publishing Co., U.S.A.*)

JACOB, GORDON (b. 1895): Quintet for cl., str. qt. (*Novello*); Diversions for wind quint., str. (*MS., O.U.P.*)

JANÁČEK, L. (1854–1928): Concertino for 2 vn., va., cl. (E flat & B flat), hn., bn., pf. (*Hudebni*)

JETTEL, R.: Trio in C minor for cl., vn., va. (*Döblinger*)

JUON, PAUL (1872–1940): Op. 18, No. 3 Trio Miniaturen for cl., vc., pf. (*Lienau*); Op. 34 Divertimento for cl., 2 va. (*Schlesinger*); Op. 27 Octet for ob., cl., hn., bn., vn., va., vc., pf. (*Schlesinger*)

KAHN, R. (1865–1951): Op. 45 Trio for cl., vc., pf. (*Schlesinger*); Op. 54 Quintet for cl., vn., hn., vc., pf. (*Böte & Bock*)

KAMINSKI, H. (1886–1946): Op. 1b Quartet for cl., va., vc., pf. (*U.E.*); Quintet for cl., hn., vn., va., vc. (*U.E.*)

KELTERBORN: Lyrische Kammermusik for cl., vn., va. (*U.E.*)

KERR, HARRISON: Trio for cl., vc., pf. (*New Music, N.Y.*)

KHACHATURIAN, A. (b. 1903): Trio for cl., vn., pf. (*B. & H.*)

KNAB, ARMIN: Lindegger Ländler for cl., vn., vc., pf. (*Schott*)

KOETSIER, JAN: Op. 13, No. 2 Trio for cl., vc., pf. (*Donemus*)

KORNAUTH, E. (b. 1891): Op. 31 Nonet for fl., ob., cl., hn., str. qt. (*U.E.*); Op. 33 Quintet for cl., str. qt. (*Döblinger*)

KREHL, S. (1864–1924): Op. 19 Quintet for cl., str. qt. (*Simrock*)

KREJCI, ISA (b. 1904): Trio for cl., db., pf. (*Artia*)

KREIN, A. A.: Op. 12 Esquisses hébraïques, 1 & 2, for cl., str. qt., 1914 (*Jurgenson*)

KŘENEK, ERNEST (b. 1900): Trio for cl., vn., pf. (*A.M.P.*)

KREUTZER, CONRADIN (1780–1849): Op. 62 Grand Septet in E flat for cl., bn., hn., vn., va., vc., db. (*Chester*)

KROMMER, F. (1759–1831): Op. 70 & 80 2 Concertinos for fl., cl., vn., va., 2 hn., vc. (*Schlesinger*)

LABOR, J. (1842–1924): Op. 11 Quintet for cl., vn., va., vc., pf. (*U.E.*)

LANDRÉ, G.: Vier Miniaturen for cl., str. qt. (*Donemus*)

LANGE, H. (b. 1884): Quintet for ob., cl., vn., va., vc. (*M.R.*)

LEERINK, HANS: Trio for cl., va., vc. (*Donemus*); Op. 19 Sonata for cl., vc. (*Donemus*)

LEEUW, TON DE (cont. Dutch): 5 Sketches for ob., cl., bn., vn., va., vc. (*Lengnick*)

LEFÈVRE, X. (1763–1829): Sonates 2 & 3 for cl., pf. with opt. vc. (*Richli*)

LOKSHIN, A.: Quintet for cl., str. qt. (*M.R.*)

LUCAS, LEIGHTON (b. 1903): Rhapsody for 2 fl., 2 cl., hp., str. qt. (*MS.*)

LUTYENS, ELISABETH (b. 1906): Op. 8, No. 5 Concerto Grosso for cl., sax., str. qt., pf. (*Chester*)

MACONCHY, ELIZABETH (b. 1907): Reflections for ob., cl., vn., hp. (*O.U.P.*)

MARKEVITCH. I. (b. 1912): Serenade for cl., vn., bn. (*Schott*); Galopp for ob., cl., bn., trpt., vn., vc., pf., perc. (*Schott*)

MARTEAU, H. (1874–1934): Op. 13 Quintet for cl., str. qt. (*Alsbach*)

MARTELLI: Concertino for ob., cl., hn., bn. & str. (*M.R.*)

MARTINU, B. (1890–1959): La Revue de Cuisine, for cl., bn., trpt., vn., vc., pf. (*Leduc*); Serenade No. 1 for cl., hn., 3 vn., va. (*B. & H.*); Serenade No. 4 for ob., cl., 4 vn., vc. (*B. & H.*); Rondi for ob., cl., bn., trpt., 2 vn., pf. (*B. & H.*); Serenade for 2 cl., vn., va., vc. (*Schott*)

MASON, D. G. (1873–1953): Op. 8 Pastorale for cl., vn., pf. (*Salabert*)

MASSENET, J. (1842–1912): Introduction and Variations for wind quint., str. qt. (*Heugel*)

MERIKANTO, AARRE (1893–1958): Concerto for vn., cl., hn., str. sextet (*Schott*)

MESSIAEN, O. (b. 1908): Quatuor pour la Fin du Temps for cl., vn., vc., pf. (*Durand*)

MIGOT, G. (b. 1891): Le 1er Livre de Divertissements français for fl., cl., hp. (*Leduc*); Quartet for fl., cl., vn., hp. (*Leduc*)

MILHAUD, D. (b. 1892): Suite for cl., vn., pf. (*Salabert*)

MIRANDOLLE, L. (cont. French): Octet for cl., hn., bn., 2 vn., va., vc., db. (*MS.*)

MOLNAR, ANTAL (b. 1890): Serenata for cl., vn., hp. (*Suvini Zerboni*)

MOÓR, E. (1863–1931): Op. 101 Double Quintet for fl., ob., cl., hn., bn., 2 vn., va., vc., db. (*Salabert*)

MOZART, W. A. (1756–91): K. 498 Trio for cl., va., pf.; K. 581 Quintet for cl., str. qt.

MUL, JAN: Quintet for cl., bn., vn., va., vc. (*Donemus*)

MULDER, ERNEST W.: Fuga III from 'Ars contrapuntica' for ob., cl., bn., vn., va., vc. (*Donemus*); Fuga IV from 'Ars contrapuntica' for fl., ob., cl., hn., 2 vn., va., vc., db. (*Donemus*)

MÜLLER, SIGFRID WALTHER: Op. 13 Divertimento for cl., str. qt. (*Br. & H.*)

MULLER-ZURICH, PAUL (b. 1898): Op. 8 Marienleben: Eight Pieces for Chamber Music for fl., ob., cl., hn., & str. qt. (*Schott*)

MUSGRAVE, THEA (b. 1928): Serenade for fl., cl., va., vc., hp. (*Chester*); Chamber Concerto for 9 instruments for ob., cl., bn., hn., trpt., tromb., vn., va., vc. (*Chester*)

NERUDA, FRANZ (1843–1915): Op. 31 Musikalische Märchen for cl., va., vc. (*Hansen*)

NIELSEN, CARL (1865–1931): Serenata-Invano for cl., hn., bn., vc., db. (*Skandinavisk*)

NØRGÅRD, PER: Op. 15 Trio for cl., vc., pf. (*Hansen*)

ONSLOW, G. (1784–1853): Nonet for wind quint., str. qt. (*Kistner*)

PEIXE, GUERRA: Music for 9 Instruments for fl., cl., bn., trpt., tromb., vn., va., vc., pf. (*Schott*)

PETRASSI, GOFFREDO (b. 1904): Sonata da Camera for fl., ob., cl., bn., 2 vn., 2 va., vc., db., harpsichord (*Suvini Zerboni*)

PETYREK, F. (1892–1951): Sextet for cl., str. qt., pf. (*U.E.*)

PFITZNER, H. (1869–1949): Op. 55 Sextet for cl., vn., va., vc., db., pf. (*Oertel*)

PICHL, W. (1741–1804): Op. 16 Three Quartettes, for cl., vn., va., vc. (*Longman*)

PITTALUGA: Ricercare for vn., cl., bn., trpt. (*Leduc*)

PLUISTER, SIMON: Divertimento for 2 fl., ob., cl., bn., hn., trpt., tromb., db., perc. (*Donemus*)

PONSE, LUCTOR: Quintet for fl., ob., cl., va., vc. (*Donemus*)

POULENC, F. (1899–1963): Rhapsodie Nègre for fl., cl., str. qt. (voice *ad lib.*), pf. (*MS., Chester*)

POUSSEUR, HENRI: Quintet for cl., bcl., pf., vn., va., hp. (*Suvini Zerboni*)

PRAAG, HENRI C. VAN: Divertimento for vl., wind quint. (*Donemus*); Wind quintet 1938 ((*Donemus*); Wind quintet 1948 (*Donemus*); Dixtuor for Wind quint., str. qt., db. (*Donemus*); Quatre réflexions for vn., wind quint. (*Donemus*); Prelude, Intermezzo & Scherzo for cl., vc. (*Donemus*)

PROKOFIEV, S. (1891–1953): Op. 39 Quintet for ob., cl., vn., va., db. (*Gutheil*); Op. 34 Overture on Yiddish Themes for cl., str. qt., pf. (*B. & H.*)

PROSPERI, C.: Four Inventions for cl., vn., va., hp. (*M.R.*)

RABL, WALTER: Op. 1 Quartet for cl., vn., vc., pf., 1897 (*Simrock*)

RAPHAEL, G. (b. 1903): Op. 4 Quintet for cl., str. qt. (*Simrock*); Op. 70 Trio for cl., vc., pf. (*B. & H.*)

RAVEL, M. (1875–1937): Introduction and Allegro for fl., cl., str. qt., hp. (*Durand*)

RAWSTHORNE, ALAN (b. 1905): Quartet for cl., vn., va., vc. (*O.U.P.*)

REGAMEY, K. (b. 1907): Quintet for cl., bn., vn., vc., pf. (*Polish State Publishing House*)

REGER, MAX (1873–1916): Op. 146 Quintet for cl., str. qt. (*Peters*)

REICHA, A. (1770–1836): Op. 96 Octet for ob., cl., bn., hn., & str. qt. (*Janet*); Quintet for cl., str. qt. (*M.R.*)

REINECKE, C. (1824–1910): Op. 264 Trio for cl., va., pf. (*Simrock*)

REIZENSTEIN, FRANZ (b. 1911): Theme & Variations for cl., str. qt. (*Lengnick*)

RHEINBERGER, J. G. (1839–1901): Op. 139 Nonet for wind quint., str. qt. (*Kistner*)

RIES, F. (1784–1838): Op. 28 Trio for cl., vc., pf. (*Simrock*); Septet for cl., hn., bn., vn., va., vc., pf. (*Probst*); Op. 128 Octet for cl., hn., bn., vn., va., vc., db. (*Kistner*)

RIETHMÜLLER, H.: Op. 46 Trio for cl., vn., pf. (*M.R.*)

RIISAGER, K. (b. 1897): Sonata for fl., cl., vn., vc. (*Hansen*)

ROETSCHER, KONRAD: Op. 22 Divertimento for fl., cl., vn., vc. (*Schott*)

ROMBERG, A. J. (1767–1821): Op. 57 Quintet for cl., vn., 2 va., vc. (*Peters*)

ROOTHAM, C. (1875–1938): Septet for wind quint., va., hp.

ROSEN, J.: Sonata for cl., vc. (*M.R.*)

RÖTSCHER, KONRAD: Op. 22 Divertimento for fl., cl., vn., vc., 1952 (*Schott*)

RUBINSTEIN, A. (1830–94): Op. 9 Octet for fl., cl., hn., vn., va., vc., pf. (*Peters*)

RUYNEMAN, D. (b. 1886): Divertimento for fl., cl., hn., va., pf. (*Chester*)

SAMAZEUILH, G. (b. 1877): Divertissement and Musette for wind quint., str. qt. (*Durand*)

SAUGUET, H. (b. 1901): Près du Bal for fl., cl., bn., vn., pf. (*Salabert*)

SCHAT, PETER: Septet for fl., ob., bcl., hn., vc., pf., perc. (*Donemus*)

SCHISKE, K. (b. 1916): Sextet for cl., str. qt., pf. (*U.E.*); Op. 27 Music for cl., trpt., va. (*U.E.*)

SCHOECK, O. (b. 1886): Op. 1 Serenade for wind quint., str. qt. (*Hug*)

SCHÖNBERG, A. (1874–1951): Op. 29 Suite for 2 cl., bcl., vn., va., vc., pf. (*U.E.*); Op. 26 Wind quintet (*U.E.*)

SCHOLLUM, R. (b. 1913): Op. 63 Octet in eight Sketches for fl., ob., cl., bn., vn., va., vc., db. (*Döblinger*)

SCHUBERT, F. (1797–1828): Op. 166 Octet for cl., hn., bn., str. qt., db.

SCHUBERT, KURT: Quintet for cl., str. qt. (*M.R.*)

SCHUMANN, R. (1810–56): Op. 132 Märchenerzählungen for cl., va., pf. (*Br. & H.*)

SCOTT, CYRIL (b. 1879): Trio for cl., vc., pf. (*MS., Elkin*)

SEARLE, HUMPHREY (b. 1915): Op. 12 Quartet for cl., bn., vn., va. (*Hinrichsen*); Variations and Finale for 10 Instruments, for wind quint., str. qt., db. (*Schott*)

SEIBER, MÁTYÁS (1905–60): Divertimento for cl., str. qt. (*MS.*)

SEKLES, B. (1872–1934): Op. 14 Serenade for fl., ob., cl., bn., hp., str. qt. (*MS., Goodwin & Tabb*)

SHAFFER, J.: Quintet for cl., str. qt. (*M.R.*)

SHIFRIN: Serenade for ob., cl., hn., va., pf. (*Hinrichsen*)

SMIT, LEO (b. 1921): Trio for cl., va., pf. (*Donemus*)

SMITH, WILLIAM O.: Suite for cl., vn. (*O.U.P.*)

SOMERVELL, A. (1863–1937): Quintet for cl., str. qt. (*MS.*)

SPOHR, L. (1784–1859): Op. 34 Andante and Variations for cl., str. qt. (*Schmidt*); Op. 31 Nonet for wind quint., str. qt. (*Litolff, Costallat*); Op. 32 Octet for cl., 2 hns., vn., 2 vas., vc., db. (*Costallat*); Op. 147 Septet for fl., cl., hn., bn., vn., vc., pf. (*Peters*); Op. 81 Fantasie with variations for cl., str. qt. (*Schmidt*)

STAMITZ, CARL (1746–1801): Op. 8 Six Quatuors, including Rococo Quartets in D and A for cl., vn., va., vc. (*McGinnis & Marx*); Quartet in E flat for cl., vn., va., vc. (*M.R.*)

STANFORD, C. V. (1852–1924): Op. 95 Serenade for fl., cl., 2 bn., hn. & str. (*S. & B.*)

STILLMAN, MICHEL: Fantasy on a Chassidish Theme for cl., str. qt. & pf. (*Edition Jibneh, Vienna*)

STOLZENBERG, G. (nineteenth–twentieth century): Op. 6 Sextet for cl., 2 vn., va., vc., db. (*Br. & H.*)

STRÄSSER, E.: Op. 34 Quintet for cl., str. qt., 1920 (*Simrock*)

STRAVINSKY, I. (b. 1882): Pastorale for vn., ob., cor ang., cl., bn. (*Schott*); Septet for cl., hn., bn., vn., va., vc., pf. (*B. & H.*); Suite de l'Histoire du Soldat (*Chester*); Eight Instrumental Miniatures for 15 players for 2 fl., 2 ob., 2 cl., 2 bn., hn., 2 vn., 2 va., 2 vc. (*Chester*); Epitaphium for fl., cl., hp. (*B. & H.*)

STURMER, BRUNO: Op. 9 Suite in G minor for 9 Instruments for fl., ob., cl., bn., str. quint. (*Schott*)

TÄGLICHSBECK, T. (1799–1867): Op. 44 Quintet for cl., str. qt. (*Heinrichshofen*)

TAILLEFERRE, G. (b. 1892): Images for fl., cl., str. qt., pf. & celeste (*Chester*)

TAK, P. C.: Duo for fl., cl., str. quint. (*Donemus*)

TARP, E. (b. 1908): Serenade for fl., cl., vn., va., vc. (*Dania*)

TATE, PHYLLIS (b. 1911): Sonata for cl., vc. (*O.U.P.*); Air & Variations for cl., vn., pf. (*O.U.P.*)

THILMAN, J.: Op. 73 Quintet for cl., str. qt. (*M.R.*)

THOMPSON, R. (b. 1899): Suite for ob., cl., va. (*Schirmer*)

TOCCHI, GIAN LUCA (b. 1901): Arlecchino: Divertimento for fl., cl., vn., va., vc., hp. (*Schott*)

TOCH, ERNST (b. 1887): Op. 30 Dance Suite in 6 Parts for fl., cl., vn., va., db., perc. (*Schott*)

TURCHI, GUIDO (b. 1916): Trio *Fra Jacopino* for fl., cl., va. (*Hinrichsen*)

UHL, ALFRED (b. 1909): Kleines Konzert for cl., va., pf. (*Döblinger*)

VILLA-LOBOS, H. (1887–1959): Choros No. 7 for fl., ob., cl., sax., bn., vn., vc. (*Schott*)

VOGEL, WLADIMIR (b. 1896): 12 Varietudes for fl., cl., vn. (*Suvini Zerboni*)

WAGNER, R. (1813–83): Adagio for cl., str. quint. (*Br. & H.*)

WALTHEW, R. (1872–1951): Quintet for cl., str. qt. (*MS.*)

WANHAL, J. (1739-1813): Op. 20 Trio in E flat No. 5 for cl., vn., pf. (& vc. or bn.) (*Schott*)

WEBER, C. M. (1786–1826): Op. 34 Quintet for cl., str. qt.; Introduction, Theme and Variations for cl., str. qt.

WEBERN, ANTON (1883–1945): Op. 22 Quartet for vn., cl., sax., pf. (*U.E.*); Op. 24 Konzert for fl., ob., cl., hn., trpt., tromb., vn., va., pf. (*U.E.*)

WEINGARTNER, F. (1863–1942) Op. 50 Quintet for cl., vn., va., vc., pf. (*Br. & H.*)

WELLESZ, E. (b. 1885): Op. 67 Octet for cl., hn., bn., str. qt., db. (*Lengnick*); Op. 81 Quintet for cl., str. qt. (*Hinrichsen*)

WESTERGAARD, SVEND: Quartet for vn., cl., vc., vibraphone (*Schott*)

WHITE, F. H. (b. 1884): Clarinda's Delight for fl., ob., cl., 2 hn., perc. (*Curwen*)

WOOLDRIDGE, JOHN: 3 Pieces for vc., fl., ob., cl., bn. (*De Wolfe*)

WURMSER, LEO (cont. British): Quintet in C for cl., str. qt. (*MS.*)

WORDSWORTH, WILLIAM (b. 1908): Quintet for cl., str. qt. (*Lengnick*)

YUN, ISANG: Music for 7 Instruments for wind quint., vn., vc. (*Schott*)

ZEMLINSKY, A. (1872–1942): Op. 3 Trio for cl., vc., pf. (*Simrock*)

ZILCHER, HERMANN (1881–1948): Trio for cl., vc., pf. (*Müller*)

VOICE WITH CLARINET, ETC.

APIVOR, DENIS (b. 1916): Op. 15 Landscapes for tenor, fl., cl., hn., vn., va., vc. (*MS.*)

APOSTEL, H. E. (b. 1901): 5 Songs for medium voice with fl., cl., bn. (*U.E.*)

BAUSSNERN, W. VON (1866–1931): Kammergesänge for high voice, str. qt., fl., cl. (*Schott*)

BERIO, LUCIANO (b. 1925): Chamber Music (James Joyce) for female voice, cl., vc., hp. (*Hinrichsen*)

BLISS, ARTHUR (b. 1891): Two Nursery Rhymes for soprano, cl., pf. (*Chester*)

BONNER, EUGÈNE (b. 1889): Flutes (4 Songs) for medium voice, fl., cl., bn., hp. (or pf.) (*Chester*)

CHERUBINI, L. (1760–1842): Ave Maria for voice, cl. (*Diabelli*)

COOKE, ARNOLD (b. 1906): Three Songs of Innocence (William Blake) for soprano, cl., pf. (*O.U.P.*)

DALLAPICCOLA, L. (b. 1904): Goethe-Lieder for mezzo-soprano, E flat cl., B flat cl., bcl. (*Suvini Zerboni*); Due Liriche di Anacreonte for soprano, E flat cl., A cl., va., pf. (*Suvini Zerboni*)

EISLER, H. (b. 1898): Op. 5 Palmström for voice, fl., cl., vn., vc. (*U.E.*)

FERRO, PIETRO: Suite Agreste for female voice, fl., cor ang., cl., va., hp. (*Ricordi*)

GAVEAUX, P. (1761–1825): Polacca from Le Trompeur trompé for voice, cl. (*Broekmans*)

GUGLIELMI, P.: Gratias agimus, for voice, cl., 1865 (*Lonsdale*)

HINDEMITH, PAUL (b. 1895): *Die Junge Magd* for contralto, fl., cl., str. qt. (*Schott*)

HUBER, K. (b. 1924): 'Des Engels Anredung an die Seele' Cantata for tenor, fl., cl., hn., hp. (*U.E.*)

HUGHES, H. (1882–1937): Three satirical songs for voice, fl., vn., cl., bn. (*Enoch*)

JACOB, GORDON (b. 1895): Three songs for soprano, cl. (*O.U.P.*)

KAMINSKI, H. (1886–1946): Three Sacred Songs for voice, cl., vn. (*U.E.*)

LLOYD, CHARLES (1849–1919): Annette, song for baritone, cl., pf. (*Novello*)

MACFARREN, G. A. (1813–87): Two songs for voice, cl. (*Chappell*)

MELLERS, WILFRID (b. 1914): Carmina filium for voice, cl., vn., vc., pf. (*MS.*)

MOZART, W. A. (1756–91): 'Parto' (La Clemenza di Tito), arr. for voice, cl., pf. (*Schott*); K. 346, 436, 439, 549 Four Notturni for 2 sopranos and bass, with 3 basset-horns (*Br. & H.*); K. 437, 438 Two Notturni for 2 sopranos and bass, with 2 cl., basset-horn (*Br. & H.*)

MUSGRAVE, THEA (b. 1928): Four Portraits for baritone, cl., pf. (*Chester*)

ORREGO SALAS, J.: Five Canciones Castellanas for voice, fl., cor ang., cl., hn., hp., perc. (*Chester*)

PETYREK, F. (1892-1951): Der Wind, for voice, cl., vn., va., pf. (*U.E.*)

POULENC, F. (1899–1963): Rhapsodie Nègre for medium voice (*ad lib.*), fl., cl., str. qt. (*MS., Chester*)

RAVEL, M. (1875–1937): 3 Poems of Mallarmé for voice, pf., str. qt., 2 fl. (picc.), cl., bcl. (*Durand*)

SAUVREZIS, A. (nineteenth–twentieth century): Hermoine et les bergers (Recitation) for baritone, fl., cl. (*Senart*)

SCHÖNBERG, A. (1874–1951): Op. 21 Pierrot Lunaire, for reciter, pf., fl., cl., vn., vc. (*U.E.*); Op. 24 Serenade for cl., bcl., mandolin, guitar, vn., va., vc., bass voice (*U.E.*)

SCHUBERT, F. (1797–1828): Der Hirt auf dem Felsen, for soprano, cl., pf. (*Augener*); Op. 46 Offertorium, for soprano, cl. (*Br. & H.*); Romanze from Die Verschworenen (Ed. Fritz Spiegl) for soprano, cl., pf. (*O.U.P.*)

SEIBER, MÁTYÁS (1905–60): Morgenstern-Lieder for soprano, cl. (*U.E.*)

SPOHR, L. (1784–1859): Op. 103 Sechs Deutsche Liede for soprano, cl., pf. (*Br. & H.*)

STRAVINSKY, I. (b. 1882): Berceuses du Chat, for contralto and 3 cl. (E flat, B flat & A) (*Chester*); Trois Poésies for voice, pf., fl., cl., str. qt. (*Ed. Russe*); Pribaoutki for medium voice, fl., ob., cl., bn., str. qt. (*MS., Chester*); Chanson sans Paroles for voice, ob., cor ang., cl., bn. (*Schott*)

TATE, PHYLLIS (b. 1911): Songs of Sundry Natures for voice, fl., cl., bn., hn., hp. (*O.U.P.*)

TEED, ROY: Five Funny Songs for baritone, cl., pf. (*MS.*)

VAUGHAN WILLIAMS, R. (1872–1958): Three Vocalises for soprano, cl. (*O.U.P.*)

VILLA-LOBOS, H. (1887–1959): Poêma da Criança e sua Mamâ, for voice, fl., cl., vc. (*Eschig*)

WALTON, WILLIAM (b. 1902): Façade, for Reciter, fl., cl., sax., trpt., vc., perc. (*O.U.P.*)

WEBERN, ANTON (1883–1945): Op. 14 Six Songs for voice, cl., bcl., vn., vc. (*U.E.*); Op. 16 Five Canons for voice, cl., bcl.

(*U.E.*); Op. 18 Three Songs for voice, cl., & guitar (*U.E.*); Op. 8 Two Songs (R. M. Rilke) for voice, cl., hn., trpt., vn., va., vc., hp. & celesta (*U.E.*); Op. 15 Sacred Songs for soprano, vn. (va.), fl., cl., trpt., hp. (*U.E.*); Three Traditional Rhymes for voice, vn. (va.), cl., bcl. (*U.E.*)

WILDGANS, F. (b. 1913): Rhénane D'Automne for soprano, cl., pf. (*U.E.*)

WILKINSON, M. (b. 1929): 'Voices' for voice, fl., cl., bcl., vc. (*U.E.*)

WEILL, K. (1900–50): Op. 10 Frauentanz for soprano, fl., va., cl., hn., bn. (*U.E.*)

Date Due